THE REVENUE RAMP

**HOW TO JUMP-START YOUR DEMAND
ENGINE TO ACCELERATE REVENUE**

LISA COLE

Hardcover ISBN: 978-1-7364334-0-9
Paperback ISBN: 978-1-7364334-5-4

Ebook ISBN: 978-1-7364334-2-3

Audiobook: 978-1-7364334-4-7

First paperback edition February 2021.

Edited by Jennifer Burgess
Layout by Ljiljana Pavkov
Cover art by Studio02

Published by Demand Accelerated, LLC

For my person, Lindsey.

*While she may not read it,
she certainly inspired it.*

TABLE OF CONTENTS

> Your team is unintentionally undermining your ability to build a Revenue RAMP to help your organization accelerate revenue. This chapter will help you prepare your team to make smart decisions as their environment rapidly evolves around them.

> Because of disjointed technologies and broken processes, your organization is wasting most of the demand it creates. This chapter will teach you how to secret shop your organization to find leaks in your response channels and key hand-offs along the lead lifecycle.

> *When organizations are under revenue pressure, leadership pushes hard for more marketing activities and leads without understanding the negative consequences for prospective customers. Marketers must create awareness for the unintended consequence of quantity over quality to gain some relief from relentless focus on activities over impact. Marketing can't go it alone. This chapter helps you create an easy to remember, compelling rallying cry that will turn critics into supporters that have your back when you're not in the room.*

> *Accelerating your company's revenue recovery will require close alignment between Marketing and Sales. To do that, you'll need to get real about how each group perceives its relationship with the other then directly address the gaps. This chapter will provide you with the tools you need to learn how sales and marketing team members perceive the working relationship with each other and develop a roadmap to measurably improve alignment.*

> *Once you've improved alignment with Sales and gained buy-in for changing focus from quantity to quality, you'll need to identify your organization's greatest opportunities to improve conversion rates. This chapter will help you assess the maturity of your sales & marketing processes, establish improvement priorities and decide on an order of operations to effectively manage change and quickly improve your organization's ability to convert demand into revenue.*

Marketing and Sales misalignment often comes down to people discussing the same things with different terminology. This chapter will show you how to gain universal acceptance for the definition of a qualified, sales-ready lead. It will also show you how to create an environment of collaboration, partnership, and accountability with the development of a mutual Service Level Agreement (SLA). Organizations that invest the time to develop and implement SLAs have measurably improved alignment and accelerate revenues as compared with organizations operating without a common language or an SLA.

To implement the SLA and enable everyone to maximize lead conversion, changes will likely need to be made to the Marketing and Sales lead management workflows. These changes will need to be enabled by technology and supported with training and communications to ensure adoption. This chapter will help you translate your new SLA into business and functional requirements to help your IT partners build or optimize your lead management engine. Additionally, this chapter will provide you with tips on how to support the team through initial go-live and full roll-out of the changes to maximize marketing and sales adoption.

In order to create the needed runway to drive meaningful change for your organization, you need to jump start your demand engine and produce some quick wins for Sales. Most organizations already have the demand they need to jump start their engine. This chapter will help you identify and recycle the dropped, ignored, stalled or lost demand that currently exists in your revenue pipeline.

Chapter 9:
Invest in Sales Productivity125

There is no more profitable investment than investing in Sales' ability to convert the leads Marketing generates. This chapter will help you identify and leverage existing assets to enable Sales. This chapter will help you identify and leverage Marketing's existing assets to enable Sales.

Phase 4: PROPEL133

Chapter 10:
Eliminate Random Acts of Marketing for Impact135

To maximize the impact and return on marketing investments, marketers will need to see, plan, execute and invest differently. This chapter will show you how to prevent random acts of marketing and build an always-on engine to create more demand with less effort.

Chapter 11:
Prove Your Impact141

For Marketing to be viewed as business drivers, your ability to establish clear linkage between investments and revenue is critical. This chapter will provide you with a measurement framework that will enable your team to manage the business of marketing and prove business impact for non-marketing stakeholders.

Conclusion149
Index159

THE
REVENUE
RAMP

INTRODUCTION

2020. The year the world stopped turning. Businesses and schools shut down. Millions of employees moved from captive office environments to working from home overnight. We stopped traveling. Economies came to a screeching halt as many companies and consumers stopped spending money on anything that was viewed as non-essential. For those that continued to spend out of necessity, buying behaviors changed dramatically. Cash became king as we all sought to weather the storm brought on by the pandemic.

A perfect storm for marketers. Experienced, talented, respected marketers lost their jobs or dealt with significant budget cuts. Marketers that retained their positions and protected their budgets faced a real crisis of confidence, paralyzed by the fear of making the wrong decisions leading them to suspend marketing initiatives waiting for the world to quickly reopen. (That quick recovery never came.) Some marketers doubled down on what they had already planned even if it no longer aligned with what buyers needed. While other marketers waited for everything to return to normal, a few bold marketers seized the opportunity to hit the reset button, refresh their strategies, and place new bets to leapfrog their competitors.

When the world stopped turning, I did a few things. First, I made sure that my own organization's house was in order, accelerated the investments that would fix all leaks in our funnel, support our customers' new buying process and enable our salesforce to shift from in-person to virtual conversations and events. While we were making the right investments and accelerating the work that would have the greatest impact, I reached out to my peers to understand what they were going to do to weather the storm. I also tuned into what the world's leading research analyst firms were sharing to help marketers respond to the rapidly changing economic environment. I consumed everything—looking for any magic bullets that would make it easier to lead through the craziness. I wanted to make sure that we didn't miss any opportunity to support the business and return to growth. I quickly realized two things. First, there is no such thing as a magic bullet. Secondly, the framework I've used repeatedly to transform marketing functions into revenue engines seemed to be the very thing marketers would need to lead their company's recovery and return to growth. Knowing that many marketers would be looking for help, I decided to publish this book that I started writing many years ago. While I don't know you, I suspect you've checked this book out for the very reasons that I finally decided to publish it:

You are under a lot of pressure from senior executives to do more to help Sales to accelerate your organization's return to growth. You know the answer cannot simply be "do more" and even if you had more to give, you're worried that you wouldn't be able to prove that Marketing was a driver of that growth.

Even though there are already tons of marketing leads that are being dropped, mishandled, or ignored altogether, you are being pushed to generate more leads to fuel an increasingly weak sales pipeline.

While sales leaders are more open to working with you out of desperation, it feels like they expect you to be their sales support versus what you are, which is a critical driver of the business.

Your team has resorted to doing more low-cost marketing activities that tend to generate lower quality leads simply to get some short-term relief from the pressure.

Your team is starting to show signs that they are stretched too thin because of the increasing number of support requests from Sales.

Finance has reduced or frozen your budget at least once this year to bring costs in line with declining revenue driven by the challenging economic downturn. Those budget cuts may have resulted in the need to lay off some of your team or terminate an agency contract.

On top of the budget cuts or freezes, you may have also lost precious marketing dollars on event cancellations.

As you develop your marketing plan, you believe that your budget will either be flat or reduced to keep costs in line with expected revenues. Despite a potential flat or decreased budget, you expect that your key performance goals will be raised to help the business return to growth. Effectively, you are being asked to do more with fewer resources.

The reliability of your marketing reports and the quality of marketing-generated leads have been called into question— may have even been blamed for the weak pipeline and missed forecasts.

Because of all these things, you are beginning to worry that you are losing credibility as a business driver and that your organization is now viewed as a cost center.

Does any of this sound familiar? Does this describe you and your situation? If so, this book is perfect for you.

According to Forrester research, top performing organizations convert less than 1.54% of leads into revenue. As if that wasn't bad enough, underperforming organizations convert less than 0.38% of leads![1] Consequently, it's not surprising to hear that less than half the CFOs McKinsey surveyed believe that Marketing delivers on

---

[1] Wizdo, L, (2013) Metrics That Matter In Lead-to-Revenue Management. Forrester. Retrieved from: https://services.forrester.com/staticassets/forresterDotCom/Webinars/2013/03/ppt/Webinar_032613_Wizdo.ppt

the promise of driving growth, and 40% don't think marketing investments should be protected during a downturn[2]. These findings were further validated by Gartner's recent surveys of CFOs indicating marketing budgets were cut by 11-25% in 2020 and that further cuts can be expected if businesses don't rebound heading into 2021.[3] The takeaway: If Marketing wants to be viewed as a business driver and profit center, we've got to generate a stronger return on our investments. The best way to do that is to improve the conversion of the demand you're already creating.

If you follow the steps outlined in this book, you and your team will quickly build a Revenue RAMP to enable your business to return to growth. This book will help you find and fix the leaks in your revenue pipeline, change Sales' perception of Marketing and the leads that Marketing generates, unlock the true potential of your marketing organization, and become omnipresent for your buyers with always-on digital marketing programs.

Let's talk about what happens after you've done this work. What will it feel like to be a marketer who is viewed as a critical business driver for their organization?

As much as I'd love to tell you that it's all rainbows, unicorns, life-changing promotions, and unlimited marketing budgets, that's a fantasy. Yes, it may happen for

[2] Boudet, J., Cvetanovski, B., Gregg, B., Heller, J. and Perrey, J. (2019) Marketing's moment is now: The C-suite partnership to deliver on growth. McKinsey & Company. Retrieved from: https://www.mckinsey.com/business-functions/marketing-and-sales/our-insights/marketings-moment-is-now-the-c-suite-partnership-to-deliver-on-growth

[3] Lavelle, J., Van Der Meulen, R. (2020) Gartner Survey Shows CFOs Will Make More Cost Cuts in 2020. Gartner. Retrieved from: https://www.gartner.com/en/newsroom/press-releases/2020-06-15-gartner-survey-shows-cfos-will-make-more-cost-cuts-in-2020

a small number of marketers but so does winning the lottery. I wouldn't place any bets on it.

But that's OK because the reality of what happens is much more rewarding. I know. I've seen it happen before, and I've experienced it in my own career.

It usually unfolds like this:

- First, you start to notice sales reps acknowledging that lead quality has measurably improved. The noise about Marketing filling their pipeline with junk leads starts to disappear from weekly commercial calls.
- Then, you notice sales highlighting key wins in the quarterly business reviews that were either sourced or heavily influenced by Marketing (and no one questions the data that proves that fact).
- Sales performance begins to rebound—sales velocity and conversion increase, resulting in more wins and quota achievement.
- Sales starts to ask Marketing for account insights as part of their territory or account planning process.
- Product and Sales leaders make sure that you and key members of your team are included in strategy and business planning sessions because you are viewed as a critical contributor to the discussion and the business, whereas, in the past, you were viewed as optional.
- The business returns to pre-pandemic revenue performance and sees signs of a return to profitable growth.
- You're able to prove, without controversy or doubt, that every dollar invested in Marketing, drives profitable, predictable, reliable revenue.

- When revenue pressure appears in the business, your CFO stops turning to Marketing first to look for ways to take costs out of the business.
- Marketing is viewed and highlighted as a competitive differentiator in earnings calls and annual reports.
- Your team feels empowered, valued, and impactful given the role they played in returning the business to growth.
- Your peers describe you as a unifying, collaborative partner who treats their team with respect.
- You feel trusted, respected, and greatly valued by your CEO, CFO and board of directors.
- If you share your team's success story externally, the transformational change you led for your organization may even be acknowledged by unbiased industry analysts.
- You'll start to attract extraordinarily talented marketers who want to work for and learn from you.
- Your KPIs evolve from lead quantity and cost per lead to demand conversion, marketing sourced and influenced revenues, and return on marketing investment.

I know it sounds too good to be true. You might even be wondering why I'd say it wasn't all rainbows and unicorns and then paint this amazing picture. Here's the thing, it is achievable. I have personally experienced all of this. You can do it too with just a little humility, hard work, dedication, and perseverance.

This book will teach you how to:

- Make sure that your team is aligned and able to make good decisions

- Find the leaks in your response channels and hand-offs along the lead lifecycle to prevent unnecessary waste
- Change the focus from quantity and cost to quality and business impact
- Unify Marketing & Sales with a "rise together" mentality—joint accountability for revenue growth
- Set your team up for success by securing universal agreement on what a qualified, sales-ready lead is/is not
- Assess the maturity of your marketing & sales processes to determine which changes need to be made and the order with which to make your changes to have the greatest impact in the least amount of time
- Translate business needs into technical requirements and build your enabling infrastructure
- Prepare the organization for go-live of the newly designed revenue engine
- Use the demand you've already created to jumpstart your engine
- Repurpose existing marketing assets and resources to enable your sales force to effectively pursue and convert more marketing-generated leads into revenue
- Inspire your team to see, plan, execute and invest differently to have an exponentially greater business impact
- Drive alignment on the metrics that matter, establish a clear linkage between marketing investments and revenue

Here is what this book does not include:

- A magic bullet

There is no such thing as a magic bullet. The Revenue RAMP framework outlined in this book provides you with a toolkit of strategies. The real magic is in the combination and sequencing of the execution of these strategies to unlock the potential of your organization. The Revenue RAMP helps marketing leaders quickly diagnose and jump-start their stalled demand engines without compromising the quality of marketing-generated leads, damaging their relationship with sales, or begging for more resources to generate leads.

Why listen to me? I've spent more than twenty years aligning Marketing and Sales in a meaningful, observable, and measurable way to propel organizations to new levels.

Through the years, I've identified the key change levers that transform marketing functions into accountable growth engines. I've worked with more than 45 leading B2B organizations across professional services, manufacturing, telecommunications, software, financial services, and higher education industries. This real-world experience in advising and counseling marketing and sales leaders, plus my relentless pursuit of case studies and best practices, are what make me a leader in my field.

For those of you that don't trust consultants or advisors, it might be helpful to know that I am a practitioner and coach who drinks her own Kool-Aid, having used the Revenue RAMP framework outlined in this book to transform two global marketing organizations in addition to helping many other leaders transform their marketing organizations. One of the transformations I have led resulted in sourcing more than $255M in revenues for my company and earned multiple awards including the Forrester/Sirius Decisions 2018 ROI Award,[4] as well as the DemandGen's 2018 B2B Innovative Marketer award.[5]

I'm currently leading another marketing transformation. While our work is not yet finished, I am proud to say that my team has been a key enabler in helping our organization manage through the chaos and disruption of 2020. Our future is bright, and I'm sure the work my team has done this year has positioned us well going into 2021.

Aside from my own personal experience with applying this framework, I have helped other marketers use these same strategies to accelerate their organizations' revenue growth as well. Here are some of the results they've realized:

- Head of Demand Generation Marketing delivered campaigns with a marketing lead-to-sales conversion rate of 12% versus the 4% of their peers while maintaining a cost per lead average 53% lower than peers
- Marketing Director grew pipeline dollar contribution from 4% to 25%+ of total pipeline while delivering 38% of total sales

---

[4] Schoening, E. (2018) SiriusDecisions Reveals Winners Of The 2018 ROI Awards. Demand Gen Report. Retrieved from: https://www.demandgenreport.com/features/news-briefs/siriusdecisions-reveals-winners-of-the-2018-roi-awards

[5] Demand Gen Report (2018) 2018 B2B Innovator Awards. Retrieved from: https://www1.demandgenreport.com/a/2018-b2b-innovator-awards/

- Vice President of Marketing generated more than $100M in total contract revenue via integrated marketing and sales enablement programs
- Senior Director of Marketing generated over 15,000 qualified, sales-ready leads that drove more than $1B revenue
- Senior Director of Marketing Operations & Demand Generation drove $14M pipeline boost in less than 6-months, nurtured 30K inquiries yearly and achieved 100% sales-lead acceptance rate globally
- Marketing Director increased Marketing's return on investment by optimizing lead management processes resulting in3 90% ROI
- Vice President of Marketing enabled sales team to generate an additional $24.5M in new bookings, 38% increase YOY

The relevance of these success stories with what is happening in our world is what drives my need to share what I've learned with you. I'm not saying all of this to brag, but to make a simple point: you're in good hands.

How to Use This Book

The goal of The Revenue RAMP is to create one simple outcome: to help you build a ramp that will enable your organization to quickly accelerate revenue growth. The chapters in this book are grouped into the four phases of work in The Revenue RAMP framework:

1. You'll **REVIEW** your marketing & sales processes to uncover gaps and opportunities.
2. You'll **ALIGN** Sales & Marketing around the key drivers of revenue generation.

3. You'll **MOBILIZE** your organization to quickly fix the leaks in your demand pipeline and secure quick wins.

4. You'll **PROPEL** your organization to growth by improving marketing effectiveness, filling the pipeline and maximizing conversion to drive business impact.

Executing the steps using the phased approach described in this book will help you prevent waste, improve sales conversion rates, and unlock the potential of your efforts and investments to accelerate growth. This can be accomplished all without stretching your team too thin, compromising lead quality, begging for more resources, or damaging your relationship with Sales.

Let's get started.

THE REVENUE
RAMP

Phase 1: **Review**

Reviewing your marketing & sales
processes to uncover gaps
and opportunities.

CHAPTER 1:

Establishing Operating Principles for Your Team

"An army of principles can penetrate where an army of soldiers cannot. "
— THOMAS PAYNE

Your team is unintentionally undermining your ability to build a Revenue RAMP for your organization. They're doing it because you're not giving them a clear set of operating principles to work from. Operating principles help your team easily understand what's working and what's not in real-time allowing them to be well-prepared to make smart decisions as their environment rapidly evolves around them. Transformative change requires that everyone is aligned in their thinking, as well as their actions.

Principle number one—Show don't tell.

To drive meaningful change, you've got to make it easy for your organization to walk a mile in your customers' shoes. Show the customers' experiences with your brand through pictures, videos, and feelings rather than through the marketing terminology and data. If a prospect has received 600+ emails from your organization in less than 6 months, create a visual that shows what their inbox looked like as a result of your email practices. If a prospect receives confusing or conflicting messages and offers from Marketing and Sales, ask them how they'd feel if Amazon did the same to them. If your organization is famous for slow lead follow-up, remind them how they felt when they were desperately seeking information on a solution for an important meeting, but the organization took 37 days to get back to their inquiry.

Principle number two—Do no harm.

Too many marketers send inbound leads prematurely to Sales without screening out fictitious leads, providing enough contact information or insight on how or why the lead engaged with their organization. They simply fail to consider how sending unqualified, non-sales ready leads might harm Sales' ability to achieve quota. According to Accenture and CSO Insights joint research study "Selling in the Age of Distraction,"[6] just 22 percent of sellers' time is taken up with lead generation, and only 36 percent of their average workweek is spent

[6] Angelos, J., Solomon, G. and Warburton, B. (2016) Selling In The Age of Disruption. Accenture. Retrieved from: https://www.accenture.com/us-en/~/media/PDF-34/Accenture-Selling-In-The-Age-Of-Distraction.pdf

selling because of administrative and service responsibilities. To achieve quotas, every minute of every selling hour counts. Minutes spent on pursuing poor quality leads prevents sales reps from converting sales opportunities they can win. Premature lead distribution has a harmful effect on sales productivity and could result in a company missing its revenue forecasts. If you send over a lead to Sales, make sure it is the best use of their time. Do no harm.

Principle number three—Sales defines what a qualified, sales-ready lead is—not Marketing.

While good marketers understand market needs, how companies buy and which behaviors indicate sales-readiness, Marketing must let Sales define what they believe is worth pursuing. It's not that Sales is better positioned to define the requirements of a qualified sales-ready lead. It comes down to one simple fact, sending truly qualified, sales-ready leads to a sales rep that still believes marketing-generated leads are junk will be ignored. It is as simple as that. Good news though— Sales rarely ever offers more stringent requirements for leads than what marketers tend to suggest, and if you let Sales define what is worthy of pursuit, you'll be able to hold them accountable for effectively managing leads because they told you what was worthy of their time. You'll just be giving them what they asked for.

Principle number four—Leave no lead behind.

Every lead—even if it's not qualified or sales-ready—is a company asset and should be handled as such. Why?

Because most inquiries will eventually buy the solution they were searching for. If a customer is an asset, so is a lead. Consider a research study conducted by Reed Business Information about inquiry handling.[7] They evaluated 40,000 inquiries from ads and press releases in magazines serving the manufacturing marketplace with the goal of understanding when, how, and why they buy.

Not surprisingly, they found that only 11% of inquiries purchased within 90 days. What is interesting is that the study also revealed the remaining 8% of those leads did eventually purchase over the following year. When they asked the inquiries who they bought from, many of the organizations responded with they eventually bought from a different company than the one where they originally inquired. When asked why they chose to buy from a different company, the most common response was that they bought from the organization that continued to stay in touch with them. They continued to show them the love even though they weren't ready to buy. Marketers should keep this in mind, making sure that no lead is left behind because they are not ready to buy at the moment. Handle all leads as if they will eventually buy from your company. That doesn't mean you're going to send them over to Sales and say, 'Hey, just stay in touch with these people.' Sales does not have the time to nurture long-term leads. Marketing should continue to nurture long-term leads while Sales stays focused on closing deals needed to achieve their monthly and quarterly goals.

---

[7] McIntosh, M. (2018) Inquiries become sales. Are you getting your share? Mac McIntosh Incorporated. Retrieved from: https://sales-lead-experts.com/learning-center/articles/b2b-inquiry-handling/inquiries-sales/

Principle number five—Do not send anything to Sales unless THEY know exactly what to do with it.

Many marketers believe, or operate with the assumption, that sales reps intuitively know how to follow up on a lead and that it's their job to know. It's not as simple of a job as marketers tend to believe. That's a problem. When you think about what it takes to effectively follow up with a lead, there are a lot of factors. First of which, happens to be the time within which you effectively connect with the lead. Sales doesn't usually understand the influence of time on conversion rates. Secondly, when Marketing sends over a lead, they rarely pass any helpful information over with it. For example, they often don't provide all the appropriate contact information for the seller to pursue the lead. They'll send over a record, but that record may, or may not, have a phone number or email address, and if it does have an email address, it is often a fictitious email address like mickeymouse@gmail.com. You could argue these should not be viewed as leads at all, but regardless they still get sent over. Does Sales have everything that they need to follow up with the lead? Do they understand how to follow up with the lead in a way that maximizes the chance of converting that lead? Finally, it is also important to share how the lead engaged with your organization. Knowing whether or not somebody registered and attended a webinar, downloaded a piece of content from a website, or interacted with a self-assessment calculator before completing a web form can help the seller be more relevant in their follow-up to convert more leads into sales. If Marketing wants to drive business growth, you must make sure Sales is set up for success, ensuring they know why the lead is valuable and what to do with it. Don't make Sales have to research to find the lead's contact information or dig deep (20+ clicks and never-ending scrolls) in CRM to find information on the lead source and buyer engagement. Make it easy for Sales to know exactly how to pursue leads effectively.

Principle number six—Speed wins deals.

The length of time it takes Sales to pursue a lead is important in maximizing lead conversion. According to Harvard Business Review, businesses who contact a lead within the first hour are 7 times more likely to qualify the lead than businesses who respond within two hours.[8] They have found that after seven business days, the lead has completely lost its value. Speed wins. Not only does Marketing need to care about how much time it takes to identify, package, and distribute leads, Sales needs to be mindful about how quickly they attempt to reach that lead. Some of the improved lead follow up time comes with extending enabling automation to Sales. Some of the improvement comes from making sure that they only receive qualified, sales-ready leads so that they don't have to try and weed through a lot of noise. There are many simple ways to improve speed to follow up. Speed wins deals.

---

[8] Oldroyd, J., McElheran, K. and Elkington, D. (2011) "The Short Life of Online Sales Leads," Harvard Business Review. Retrieved from: https://hbr. org/2011/03/the-short-life-of-online-sales-leads

Principle number seven—There is no such thing as 50/50 relationship. Give 100%.

*"Trust is like love. Both parties have
to feel it before it really exists. "*
— SIMON SINEK

If Sales doesn't appear to want to be a partner, you must go out of your way to bring them to the table. Show them that your partnership is important and that you're willing to work to strengthen your relationship. Companies cannot grow revenue if the two core components of their revenue engine can't work together. The challenge is for you and your team to get past the likely baggage that exists between your two groups. The baggage could be specific to you. You could have inherited baggage from your predecessor, or it could be historical baggage that Sales has built over the years from different relationships with different marketing organizations. Given the potential of historical baggage between Marketing and Sales, you need to have the courage to show up first. Doing so means you are going to have to be vulnerable and reach across the aisle to help your peers. The small silver lining of challenging years and economic recessions is that people tend to be open to help and change. Everyone needs help now. If you reach across the aisle in the spirit of support and assistance, with the sole intent of helping your sales counterparts, I guarantee that they will be more receptive to Marketing help than ever before. If you let your guard down, admit that not everything is perfect, acknowledge the things that weren't working, and offer to help Sales, you will disarm and diffuse even the most strained relationships. I've seen it time and time again. Being vulnerable can disarm or diffuse even the most explosive relationships and turn skeptics into partners.

Principle eight—Automate. Automate. Automate.

Humans introduce errors and unnecessary delays into the lead lifecycle. It is especially important to automate as much of the lead handling processes as possible so that you can eliminate those errors and delays. If a lead comes in through a web form and you have everything associated with that form submit routed to someone's email inbox, there's a chance it will get dropped. If you then expect that recipient to manually assign and distribute those leads, there's a greater chance it will get mishandled. There's also the potential for those leads to get lost on the way to inboxes for people that might've left the company. When Marketing exhibits at an in-person event, there's usually a human responsible for capturing leads, manually compiling the leads into a spreadsheet then uploading them into CRM. Again, that's open to human error. There are lots of ways to capture leads and to automate the flow of data across technologies with tighter integrations. Explore solutions that send records directly to your CRM of choice and automate lead assignment and routing. Even if you find yourself having to deal with disparate, disjointed technologies, many marketers have set up RPA (robotic process automation) bots to manage all the repetitive work on those platforms for you. Robotic process automation capable of logging into one system, importing records, and/or making changes, and then copy and pasting that data to port over into another system. Removing human error, can also make you a little bit more scalable. Make sure that you know how leads enter your ecosystem, where they go and how they get converted then automate to the greatest degree possible. The goal here is improving the turnaround time on lead follow up from days and weeks of initial engagement to hours.

Principle number nine—Question everything. Assume Nothing.

Throughout this book, you'll learn about many opportunities to accelerate revenue growth for your organization. To effectively execute that growth, though, you've got to stop making assumptions. Don't assume that your team knows exactly where every lead is sent. Don't assume that you know what Sales believes a qualified, sales-ready lead should look like. Don't assume that Sales knows how to pursue a lead or has all the information they need to convert the lead. Don't assume that Sales is continuing to nurture long-term leads that may have stalled or been lost.

You're probably wondering why these principles matter. Over the last 20 years, I have seen and heard about many situations where team members, either my clients' team members or my own team members, have damaged Marketing's credibility and/or impeded their ability to lead this kind of transformational change. They did it unintentionally for sure, but they did it because they didn't realize that the details of what Marketing was trying to do or how easy it would be to lose credibility.

For example, I'll never forget the time one of my team members unintentionally blew up a sales training session by referring to a purchased list of names as leads. Purchased names of people that may or may not have ever heard of your company are not leads and they should never be treated as such. Having a member of my own team make that kind of statement during the sales training session for our new service level agreement was a problem that we had to work through. While it might seem like a small misstep, one of the sales reps picked up on it immediately and used it to question whether Marketing was really going to improve lead quality.

Another example, there was a time I facilitated a lead definition workshop for a client to help her gather what Sales viewed as a qualified, sales-ready lead and what they needed to effectively convert leads. The marketing team dominated the conversation and wouldn't let Sales answer any questions. They failed to remember that Marketing doesn't define what a qualified, sales-ready lead is, Sales does. Not only did they waste Sales' time, they damaged their relationship with Sales, as it was clear Marketing really didn't care about what Sales felt they needed to be successful.

Then there was the time that my team sat on a list of 1200 highly qualified sales-ready leads from a hugely successful webinar for more than three weeks. They sat on that list for more than three weeks because it was somebody else's job to import and assign the leads and that person was out on an unexpected leave. They assumed that when that person came back, she could handle it because it was her job. If the team had been following this operating set of principles of 'leave no

lead behind' and 'speed win deals,' those two principles would have prompted them to handle it differently
regardless of whose job it normally was. This brings us
to the last operating principle.

Principle number ten—No one is exempt from these principles.

Whether you are a lead management specialist, a creative designer, a copywriter, a marketing automation
manager, or a chief marketing officer, regardless of your
role in your organization, all the above principles apply
to every single member of your marketing team. All are
equally responsible for following these principles. Think
back on the example I gave about my team sitting on a
list of 1200 highly qualified sales-ready leads; that miss
was on me. Had I provided my team with these operating principles, they would never have left those leads
for someone else to manage. Give your team operating
principles, help them understand what's working and
what's not and make solid decisions. With these principles, they'll be well-prepared to make smart decisions
as their environment evolves around them.

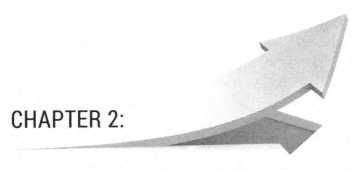

CHAPTER 2:

Inspect What You Expect.

In this chapter, I'll help you identify the leaks in your revenue pipeline that lead to wasted demand. When these leaks are identified and fixed, you'll eliminate waste, improve sales velocity, maximize lead conversion, and drive revenue growth—faster. To illustrate how impactful fixing your leaky funnel can be, I'd like to tell you a story.

Imagine an operations manager at a manufacturing company. They receive a thousand parts. Each one of those parts is worth $10,000, bringing a total value of $10 million in inventory. 200 of those parts are lost immediately. 200 of those parts are sent to the right place, but several weeks late. 200 are sent to the right place, but the employees have no idea what to do with them. 200 are defective, but there are no processes in place to fix them. The final 200 are delivered to the right employee *on time with instructions and in excellent condition.* If this continues, how long do you think the operations manager gets to keep their job? Not very long.

Now imagine a marketing leader at a business to business organization selling expensive, highly technical products. Marketing generates a thousand leads, each worth a potential sale of $100K dollars, which brings it to a total potential value of $100M dollars. 200 of those leads are immediately lost. 200 are sent to the wrong salesperson or the right salesperson, but lead follow-up takes days or weeks for various reasons. 200 are sent to the right salesperson, but they have no idea what to do with them. 200 are not qualified, but there are no processes in place to fix them. The final 200 are delivered to the right salesperson on time with clear instructions and are viewed upon arrival as qualified and sales ready.

Having wasted $80 million in potential sales opportunities, how long do you think that marketing leader would get to keep their job? Not very long, yet it happens often.

Spencer Stuart performs benchmark studies every year on the average tenure of C-suite executives. Marketing executives often have a significantly higher attrition than their peers. The average tenure of a Marketing executive right now is 41 months.[9] It's almost half of the average tenure of a CEO, a CFO, or a CIO. That is not very long. When you ask a CEO why that is, the CEO will tell you that they don't trust that Marketing really understands the business. They don't speak in

___

[9] Spencer Stuart (2020) Women & Minorities Make Significant Gains Within the CMO Ranks in 2019. Retrieved from: https://www.spencerstuart.com/research-and-insight/women-and-minorities-make-significant-gains-within-the-cmo-ranks-in-2019

the same financial terms, and they don't prove that their investments have a meaningful business impact. The most common reason for either the marketer choosing to leave on their own, or being asked to leave, is that they're unable to demonstrate a meaningful business impact. They're not viewed as business drivers. In many cases, they don't use the same language as the rest of the C-suite participants. When you think about business impact, one of the key enablers of demonstrating business impact is making sure that the awareness and demand you're creating converts into revenue. Wasted demand and inability to prove business impact is a key contributing factor to the low tenure rate of marketing executives.

Fixing your leaky revenue pipeline starts with secret shopping your organization's response channels. Secret shopping your organization means that you or a member of your network go undercover to experience what it is like to be a customer of your organization. You observe, interact, assess and report on your experiences. The goal of this assessment is to help you identify the leaks in your pipeline, eliminate waste, and streamline the processes to improve the overall timing of the lead lifecycle, maximize lead conversion, and drive meaningful business impact. The assessment includes how you capture leads, how leads are defined in terms of how qualified and sales-ready they are, how you are cleansing and enriching your data, how you're screening leads before passing them to Sales, how you're using tele-qualification to validate sales readiness, how those leads are assigned and distributed to Sales, and what is provided to them that enables lead follow up.

Leads are generated through a variety of online and offline tactics. What are all the ways that leads, or records, enter your ecosystem? What are all the sources of leads that you're generating today? How do you capture those leads? For example, if trade shows, conferences, or webinars are sources of leads for you, how are you importing the records into your CRM or marketing automation platform (MAP)?

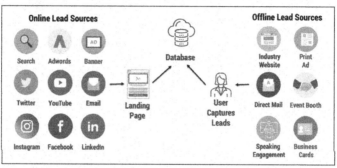

Lead Flow Diagram

What do you do with the lead once it's identified and captured? How do you know when it's appropriate to send it to Sales for follow up? What is your current definition of a qualified sales-ready lead? What lead scoring models do you have in place today that enable you to determine which leads are ready for distribution to Sales? How are you verifying and visually screening those leads before passing them on to Sales to make sure that they do in fact, meet those requirements? How are leads assigned and distributed today? What info and tools are being shared or sent along with those leads when they're passed to Sales? What actions do you expect the recipient of that lead to take once the lead has been assigned to them? What are you doing with those that are not yet viewed as qualified and sales-ready? How are you nurturing them? As leads advance from one stage to another, how are you tracking that leads are effectively passed from one function to another? Are you verifying that lead follow-up is happening? Do you know how long leads sit at each stage? What happens when leads appear to stay in one stage for a long period of time?

How are the leads assigned, routed and distributed to Sales? What do you do with the leads that have had no forward progress at all over a period of 180 days? (Remember most people that raised their hand to learn more won't buy within 90 days, but they will eventually buy within a year.) What are you doing with those leads that were disqualified or dispositioned as lost? How are you recycling them? How are you protecting leads while they're in the opportunity pipeline? How are you making sure that you don't send duplicate leads to sales reps?

How are you measuring the velocity of leads across the entire lead lifecycle? How long does it take from the initial hand raising or engagement from the prospect or the lead until Sales follows up? Do you know how good your top three competitors are with managing leads? Have you secret shopped their lead handling experience? Could this become a competitive advantage for your company?

After completing this assessment for my last organization, we learned there was very inconsistent data entry which was hindering lead follow-up. All inquiries were being sent over to Sales with little to no filtering. There was so much noise in the pipeline, it was nearly impossible to identify hot leads that had requested sales appointments. The lead assignment process was manual and inefficient. There was no real lead notification process. When leads somehow magically appeared in CRM for a sales rep, they had no idea what to do with them.

After evaluating how long it took for a lead to successfully flow from Marketing to Sales, we looked closely at all the ways we captured leads. We started with inbound phone calls. All the numbers that were listed on our site routed to either general receptionists who didn't have a plan for how to route leads, or they pointed to an unidentifiable voicemail box. Most of those voicemail boxes were either full, didn't allow for any sort of voice message, or were perpetually busy.

Once we knew what was happening to inbound phone calls and had a plan for how to fix the issues, we audited all our web forms. We clicked on all Call-To-Action (CTA) buttons on our website and tested each form. We learned that many CTA buttons didn't work and for the CTAs that did work, the web forms didn't mandate any sort of phone number, email information, or verify the validity of the form fields. We were sending leads to Sales for follow-up even though Sales had nothing they could use to pursue those leads. To make matters worse, many of the web form submits were sent directly to sales reps' email inboxes without any sort of filtering and without adding records to CRM. There was no real visibility that was maintained as the lead was identified, captured or distributed.

We also learned that most of the people that we were routing leads to were employees that were no longer with the company. Don't forget, sales organizations tend to have very high attrition due to aggressive quotas. Lead assignment rules and workflows can quickly become outdated if not managed effectively. We had more than 4,000 web inquiries in the year prior, 95% of which were sent to people that weren't there. 3800 web inquiries were lost! If our organization had effectively converted just 3% of these inquiries into sales at an average deal size of $50K, we would have generated more than $5.7 million in revenue!

On a roll, we turned our attention to how we managed our event leads. While in-person events are rare nowadays, they do drive high quantities of leads, so it's worth including in your assessment should you start to invest in in-person events in the future. We learned that over time Marketing had institutionalized the cherry-picking of leads. Sales didn't trust that Marketing would effectively follow up with leads, so they required a grace period to review the spreadsheet of leads captured at any event and claimed ownership of leads to be removed from the lead management workflow. With this added manual step, Marketing was effectively saying, "hey, please go cherry-pick through this list, so we'll know up front which leads you plan to ignore." Beyond the small handful of leads that made it through that process, virtually none were followed up on because they weren't perceived as being qualified or sales ready.

After evaluating how leads entered our system, we benchmarked the average turnaround time from initial capture to sales follow up. Our average turnaround time was 37 days! I remember inserting myself into one example of a stalled lead and found out the lead was sent to multiple reps where they were debating who would follow-up on the lead and what the best messaging would be. They agreed to schedule a team conference call to get aligned on these two questions before following up on the lead but here's the kicker, between existing meetings, planned PTO, and a holiday, they couldn't get together until the following month in order to come to an agreement on how to follow-up on the lead. While the intent was good, the result was a wasted opportunity. Your messaging will never be impactful if it takes too long to get back to the lead!

Once we knew how long lead follow-up was taking; we looked critically at the information we were passing to Sales along with the lead. We put ourselves in their shoes and tried to determine if we'd be able to effectively follow up with the lead based on the information provided. We concluded that there was not enough information to reach the lead much less have a productive conversation should we be lucky enough to connect with the lead. Best case scenario was that we'd provide the name of the person, the name of their company and either a phone number or email address. We rarely told the sales rep how the lead was generated and when we did, it sounded like this, "Hey, all your leads from XYZ event have been loaded into Salesforce." Other than that, there weren't any individual lead notifications. For a sales rep to pursue a lead, they first had to do research to prepare themselves for the discussion. While it increased the odds of converting the leads to sales, it wasted precious selling time they could have been using to close more deals.

Remember, disjointed technologies, disparate data, and broken processes are very common, as marketing technology stacks are rapidly expanding to support more advanced marketing strategies and higher customer expectations. Your organization may be wasting most of the demand it's creating, and that, in turn, leads to greater pressure to generate more leads, which then puts pressure on your team to certainly sacrifice quality to get more done, which is only further perpetuating the problem. Secret shop yourself and find where your greatest opportunities for improvement are. If you have web forms that go to people that are no longer with your company, fix them. If you have phone numbers listed throughout your site, or on brochures, that go to a general receptionist, people, or voicemails, particularly those that won't even let you leave a voice message, fix them. If you've got broken CTAs, fix them. If you've got web forms that email individuals directly, rather than flowing through your CRM, fix them. Take the time to experience your organization from your customer's perspective, document it, consolidate the entire workflow into one visual, and then use that to shape an improvement roadmap your team can quickly execute.

Five years ago, I had a strong feeling that no one had been paying attention to inbound leads and that there might be an opportunity to accelerate pipeline growth with some improvements. It turned out that 95% of all inbound channels were broken. 95% of all inbound interest was simply lost without even trying to convert it into opportunities and sales. Once we fixed the leads, there was an immediate measurable increase in pipeline revenue. It suddenly got much easier to prove business impact.

CHAPTER 3:

Create Your Wall of Shame

You're probably wondering why I'd recommend creating a wall of shame. Who suggests doing anything that brings about the feeling of shame? Stay with me on this one. It was a real game changer for me and for others.

A few years ago, I was the newly promoted marketing leader of a global management consulting firm. Before my promotion was even announced, I was asked to reduce my budget by $1M while also finding a way to increase marketing activities in order to help the business return to growth.

One of the toughest things about being a marketer in a consulting organization is that all consultants believe they are talented marketers because they were successful in building a portfolio of clients through the years. In addition to believing they're marketers, they also tend to believe in magic bullets. *Just send one more email.*

Let's go to this one event. Let's just do this one advertisement with this industry trade publication. Let's just pay this association to blast our email to their members. Let's post on LinkedIn that we're exhibiting at XYZ trade show – booth #657. If you just do this one thing for me, I'll find more opportunities. Because I am so good at closing, we'll hit our numbers. I call these 'random acts of marketing' and many sales executives are addicted to them. Addiction to random acts of marketing is hard to break especially when there's revenue pressure in the business.

When numbers are down and budgets are reduced, the tendency is to demand more email blasts or social media posts because they're believed to be free. Good marketers know there is no such thing as free. One tactic isn't going to generate the kind of results the business is expecting, and ad-hoc, one-size-fits-all tactics result in poor customer experiences. Unfortunately, many marketers spend their days trying to educate non-marketers on the negative consequences of random acts of marketing and fail to gain buy-in for thinking programmatically and prioritizing quality over quantity. This constant struggle can get very tiring and is one of the reasons why marketing leaders tend to move on from an organization. No one wants to feel relegated to some simple tactical communications or advertising activities. Meaning they had become the doers of things for their organization and not necessarily a business driver. With that dissatisfaction and feeling like they can't win, they give up and go on to a different organization in hopes that that new organization will treat them differently.

While editing this chapter, my phone blew up with notifications from LinkedIn. There were more than 30 notifications for chief marketing officer positions and 50 notifications for vice president of marketing positions that had just opened. That's 80 new marketing leadership roles opening in one city in ONE day! While some might truly be new opportunities, experience tells me that a large portion of those positions were vacated by marketers looking for a new opportunity with a company that would view them as business drivers.

It's time to share a little secret with you that has worked well for me, more than once. This secret helped me not only change sales perception of these activities but also gave my allies a rallying cry for changing or treating marketing and/or marketing investments differently.

Did you know that one poor experience can lead to one quarter of your prospects walking away? When organizations are under pressure, they tend to value quantity over quality and start delivering horrible experiences to customers. You're going to look for the worst possible examples in your database of where your organization has emailed the prospect/customer so often that you're shocked they've not unsubscribed, blacklisted, or reported you for violation of CAN-SPAM or GDPR regulations. Then you're going to take that example and shine a big light on it for all to see. This example is going to become your organization's wall of shame, the reason why your organization can't continue marketing the way they have.

I'll never forget the first time I used this strategy. We were beginning to feel overwhelmed by a growing backlog of email send requests and knew that if it were left unchecked, we'd get to a point where we wouldn't be able to keep up. I asked my team to go into our marketing database and identify the one person that's received the most emails from us. Then get back to me with a full review of the tactics they've received and their response behaviors. They found one person that within 90 days received more than 68 emails from us. I asked them to print out every email that we sent and then stick it on a large empty wall in the order that he had received them along with a post-it sticky note indicating what the response behavior was. I wanted my team to put ourselves in his shoes. Who was he? Were there too many emails? Were they consistent in messaging? Were they consistent in the look and feel? Did the offers seem to build on each other, as if we were having a conversation with him? That's it. I wanted to see the example in our database where I could hang on a physical wall, and say, "We can't just keep sending more emails thinking it's going to drive revenue."

The unwilling victim of our random acts of marketing emails was the CEO of a major health system. Not only had he received 68 emails in 90 days, but also more than 100 emails in six months. Despite all that activity, he only opened two of the emails, clicked through none of them, and bought nothing.

Those 68 emails were all different in look and feel. They could not be recognized as having been from the same organization. We had grown through acquisition and each practice operated independently. That clearly showed in our emails. The messages were not consistent. There wasn't a clear underlying thread or positioning throughout any of them. In fact, there were several offers that conflicted with each other. For example, two emails offered two hosted events in two different locations on the same day. We were sending him competing offers and no one noticed because no one was cross-referencing across all the target lists. It's a miracle that he didn't unsubscribe, didn't blacklist the organization, or report us for spam. This was a powerful exercise because that example was a visual outline of his experience with our company.

When we shared this with our stakeholder group, everyone was obviously horrified. The thought that the CEO of a top health system in the country had received these 68 conflicting, confusing emails hit home. Their response, "We hear you. We know the answer is no longer to send one off email or only care about that individual offer from an individual practice or product line. You tell us what good marketing should look like." With one photo, we immediately had the support to be more programmatic in our marketing. That same photo moved us away from being the doers of things. It was our starting point for gaining the acceptance needed to develop more advanced marketing strategies intended to drive pipeline and revenue growth—an enterprise-wide, account-based marketing strategy for strategic accounts.

One of the cool, yet unexpected, benefits of this experiment was that the wall of shame became the basis for the organization's rallying cry around being thoughtful, strategic, programmatic, and intentional in all that we do as an enterprise.

Other functional groups like IT, Finance, and HR went out to find their own walls of shame to publish. We were all suffering from the same pressure and the same attitude of 'Just do what I tell you. I don't need your group to be strategic or thoughtful or programmatic, we just want this one thing.' Every functional group had been relegated to the doer of sales things. It eventually became a framework that everyone else applied to their team's work to gain acceptance for transformational change across the board.

After successfully transforming that marketing organization and enabling the organization to return to revenue growth, I decided to pursue a new opportunity at a new organization. I joined the senior executive team as the head of corporate marketing for a global manufacturing organization. After seeing how well the wall of shame strategy worked for my previous organization, as well as a handful of others that created their own walls of shame on my recommendation, I decided that I was going find the wall of shame there right off the bat so I could gain buy-in advocacy and support for the transformational change needed to drive meaningful business impact. Sure enough, it wasn't hard to find and create a compelling wall of shame. There was a guy in the database that had received more than 600 emails from the organization in less than a year. As part of my first global, all-hands meeting where I outlined all that Marketing was going to do to support the business' new go-to-market strategy, I embedded a minute and a half video that showed what the prospect's inbox looked like over that last year loaded with my company's emails. He had received more than two emails every single day from my organization and none of those messages had any connective tissue between them. Like the previous scenario, he hadn't clicked through or bought anything. It was horrifying enough for the organization to embrace new marketing strategies and tactics.

I suggest starting with email. It's the one tactic that is fully contained within your marketing automation platform. It's the one tactic that there was a request, an activity and a result all captured within one platform—no need to aggregate across technologies. Look at the records that have received the most emails over some predefined set of time. I would start with 90 days and if you don't find a compelling wall of shame in a 90-day timeframe, expand it out. You can go to six months; you can go to one year. If you don't find such a case, the next scenario would be to find the record in the database or number of records that received only one email and look closely at the offer to see if your organization did anything to follow-up. You sent an email, they might have subscribed to further communications or asked to be contacted, and then you did nothing with them.

Believe it or not, lots of organizations send many emails to an ever-growing database, but they never return to the people that have already engaged, and they rarely have a plan for what's next from the customer or prospect's perspective. We do a lot of "ghosting" and that's equally as damaging from the customer's point of view.

If you don't find anything compelling in your email database, congratulations! You belong to one of only a few organizations that don't treat email as a magic bullet and are not beholden to free tactics, or measured by how many activities your team executes. If you still want to find a rallying cry to gain support for more of a programmatic approach to marketing, evaluate how you engage in other channels. Look in the CRM for the person who had the most touch points across all different tactic types and then work to see if you have any examples of a record that has received an excessive number of communications or wildly disjointed messages. Chances are you'll either find people that have received an extraordinary amount of activities or they've only received one and got ghosted.

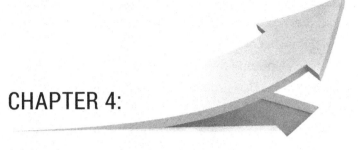

CHAPTER 4:

Sales' Perception of Marketing is YOUR Reality. Make Sure It's How YOU Want to be Viewed

If I were to ask your Sales leaders about their perception of Marketing and what influences that perception, what would they say? Do you know? If not, this chapter will help answer that question and help you uncover the source of Marketing and Sales misalignment for your organization.

While many Marketers have a gut feeling about what could be improved, few know which improvements would have the greatest impact on the relationship from Sales' perspective. The best way to learn how someone perceives their relationship with you and what could be improved is to simply ask them. We're going to conduct a mirrored survey where the same questionnaire is provided to both Sales and Marketing team members since a healthy relationship is never one-sided. You can then use the two views to identify the areas where you're most misaligned.

It is also important that you survey team members across all levels of the organization. You can't ask one sales leader or stakeholder within the sales organization how they perceive their relationship with you and assume that's representative of the collective relationship between Marketing and Sales. You'll need a complete picture of how stakeholders across the individual sales groups and at every organization level perceive their working relationship with you.

Why? In some organizations, the leaders of both Marketing and Sales are closely aligned, but at levels underneath those leaders, alignment doesn't exist. In other organizations, a marketing leader might have strong relationships with the frontline sales reps, or regional sales managers, but their relationship with the head of Sales is either subservient or non-existent. To ensure you get a reliable snapshot that you can build an action plan on, survey a sample of individuals at different levels throughout the Sales organization.

Now that we understand the overarching approach, it's time to get to work on the survey itself. The survey assesses six key areas where alignment is critical for revenue generation: organizational relationships, metrics and value measurement, demand generation, company culture, systems and technology, and messaging and materials. You will ask the same questions of both Sales

& Marketing regarding each function's goals and objectives, the way performance is measured, how demand is created and converted to revenue, whether or not your company's culture is conducive to a partnership, the systems and technologies the two groups use and how they interact with each other, the data that the integrated technologies yield, what messaging and materials are used in the market, and how those messages and materials get crafted and used.

Let's take it one area at a time, starting with organizational relationships. Within the organizational relationship section, you're trying to understand how well each function understands the other. How well does Marketing understand the sales process? How well does Sales understand marketing practices? How clear are they about who does what? Do they work together to pursue a market opportunity or to solve a business challenge? Drilling in on Marketing's understanding of sales, does marketing management lack an understanding of the sales function, process, and skill sets required to be successful? Have they been a sales rep before or managed a team of sales reps? Do they have a good understanding of the sales function? Do they encourage that same understanding amongst all the marketing staff?

What is Sales' understanding of Marketing? Does sales management lack an understanding of the marketing function? Do they have a good understanding and command of marketing best practices? Have they ever owned responsibility for marketing throughout their career journey? What is their point of view about Marketing's role in the business?

How do Sales and Marketing collaborate? Immature organizations tend to rely on random email exchanges or conference calls with very inconsistent partici-pants. In this situation, you and your team may feel as though you spend a lot of time repeating yourselves. Are there regularly occurring meetings with key staff from both functions but only for the duration of spe-cial cross-functional initiatives? Or is there a consis-tent, structured meeting between the heads of Sales and Marketing with consistent and structured meetings between team members from the next level managers of both marketing and sales functions? Is there a for-mal alignment program with widespread participation across all levels of the organizations in both Sales and Marketing? How well does the frontline of Marketing collaborate with the frontline of the Sales organiza-tion? How do they communicate with each other? Are they communicating consistently, both formally and informally? Is there a continuous feedback loop that requires both to bring information to the table?

How clear are the sales and marketing roles and responsibilities? In immature organizations, roles and responsibilities are largely undefined. The functions develop independently, and focus on their own tasks. If Marketing ceased to exist tomorrow, Sales might not notice until it showed up in the numbers. Are there efforts underway to prevent disputes, such as devel-oping a common language and clarifying roles and responsibilities? Do Marketing and Sales share mea-surement systems? Do they share performance metrics? Are they rewarded together? Is it a *"rise together or fall apart"* culture?

Finally, how strong are the relationships between the team members? Are the two groups always at odds with each other? Is there open criticism? Is there a lack of cooperation between the groups? Is finger pointing common? Or do they work together well? Do they trust each other? Do they assume positive intentions? Do they speak openly and productively during challenging times? Fact-based constructive feedback is productive. Emotional attacks based on assumptions are not productive.

Moving from organizational relationships to metrics and value measurement, how are Sales and Marketing reviewing metrics today? Are marketing metrics regularly reviewed with Sales or only Sales asks for them? Do Marketing and Sales act on insights gathered through a review of results? Is Marketing applying Sales' feedback to further optimize marketing spend?

What are the metrics used to measure performance of marketing programs and tactics? For immature organizations, there is typically a focus on marketing activity and cost metrics. Often there is a focus on cost per lead and lead quantity measures, but inconsistently reviewed with Sales. While we'll share measurement and reporting best practices in Chapter Eleven, it is important to note that an organizational focus on cost per lead as a key metric is a clear sign that Marketing is viewed as a cost center, as opposed to a business driver. Unfortunately, marketers are usually the drivers of establishing this as an important metric because they don't fully understand the unintended consequences. Focusing on cost per lead results in making decisions that negatively impact lead quality and undermine Marketing's ability to accelerate revenue growth. Marketers focused on reducing cost per lead typically favor low-cost tactics that yield a large quantity of leads and underinvest in longer-term strategies like lead nurturing and pipeline acceleration because they increase cost per lead.

Mature marketing organizations recognize the importance of lead quality and conversion, measure sourced and influenced revenues and report return on marketing investment. As organizations increasingly become customer-centric, mature marketing organizations recognize the best way to link Marketing & Sales is by aligning to customers and take the lead on measuring and acting on customer-focused metrics such as return on customer and average lifetime value of a customer.

Since the marketing pipeline will eventually reveal itself in the sales pipeline, how have you been reporting on the marketing and sales pipelines? Are they treated as two different things? Does Sales care about the marketing pipeline? Has Marketing been able to demonstrate clear cause and effect between the marketing and sales pipelines? Are you acting with one integrated view of the revenue pipeline? Has your organization used what you're seeing in the marketing pipeline to improve the reliability of revenue forecasting? Do Marketing and Sales share responsibility for the reliability of the revenue pipeline? Do they work together to improve the flow and conversion of demand through the revenue pipeline?

How reliable are your company's revenue forecasts? What role does Marketing performance play in influencing future revenue forecasts? Immature organizations often have no consistent commitment to long-term revenue forecasting, or there might be revenue forecasting, but it does not take into consideration Marketing's potential impact on those forecasts. Mature organizations have a reliable, near-real time, integrated view of both the marketing and sales pipeline that lead to predictable and reliable forecasts. Mature organizations do not have panic attacks approaching the end of every month, quarter or year because they have a reliable, integrated view of the marketing and sales pipeline.

Shifting from metrics and value measurement to the way your organization creates demand, how do you generate leads as a company? Is Marketing a sales support function while Sales develops their own leads? Does Marketing execute lead generation programs and pass leads to Sales for qualification and conversion? Does Marketing share responsibility for the conversion of leads into opportunities and sales? Mature organizations have highly synchronized demand generation programs where Marketing and Sales are all working together to source demand in an orchestrated way in order to accelerate revenue in a predictable, reliable manner.

How are you managing the leads Marketing generates? Immature marketers allow all inbound inquiries to flow right through to Sales without any sort of filtering. As marketing processes mature, leads are minimally screened to prevent fictitious or duplicative leads from being sent to Sales. Mature organizations have established a universally accepted lead definition with clear handoff processes between Marketing and Sales, as well as a closed loop feedback mechanism to continuously optimize lead handling. Advanced marketers have established processes and programs to effectively recycle stalled or lost leads, so no demand is wasted.

Let's talk about your company's culture. There is a strong possibility that your company's organizational design and culture supports Marketing and Sales alignment. This is true when Marketing and Sales report up through siloed executive leaders that aren't aligned on goals, objectives, and market priorities. Even if Marketing and Sales report to the same senior executive, misalignment could happen if that senior executive doesn't establish shared goals and objectives, engage with them separately, or encourages them to operate in silos.

How are Sales and Marketing compensated and rewarded? In immature organizations, it could be that very little risk is taken on either side. If the rewards are not tied to any sort of joint success or if it's not apparent to frontline employees how they're sharing in those rewards, alignment will feel unachievable. As an organization matures, Marketing and Sales evolve from occasionally sharing risk and rewards to consistently sharing risk and rewards with one fully integrated incentive compensation system. A common example of how rewards and compensation can prevent meaningful alignment is when Marketing is held responsible for marketing activities and lead quantity or reducing average cost per lead and Sales is responsible for driving profitable revenue growth. Marketing driving as many leads as possible into the system at the lowest possible cost will negatively impact sales productivity and ultimately keep Sales from achieving their goals. Marketing and Sales should both be on the hook for the same revenue number. If you look at the core KPIs of your organization and don't see a direct link between Marketing and revenue, you will be treated as a cost center. Go on the hook for a number, even if it feels like it is a small percentage of overall revenue. Start somewhere and then work to grow your influence. Marketing technology has advanced so quickly that Marketing can prove what percentage of the organization's revenues have been sourced or significantly influenced by a marketing investment. There are no excuses.

During moments of crisis, what happens? How do the leaders of the two functional groups respond? Do they get paralyzed by the crisis? Does each team go off on its own to generate ideas for how to respond to the crisis? In an ideal state, Sales and Marketing would work together on how to manage through the crisis, and work together to develop then execute on both the short and long-term initiatives to stabilize and grow the business. This year helped us all see what really happens in a crisis. There isn't an organization anywhere in the world that did not find themselves in a complete state of panic when entire economies around the world shut down. If you found that your team was working in a vacuum, trying to come up with ideas for how to help the business recover, and you weren't partnered with sales on those ideas, or you found out that product or sales were brainstorming ideas and didn't include you or your team, that should be a strong enough sign for you that they don't yet see you as a business driver.

Do Marketing and Sales appear to trust each other? How do you manage through conflict? Do you have a transactional relationship where you only engage with each other around a singular transaction or request and because of that, you only have conflict occasionally? As Marketing and Sales begin to trust each other, Marketing becomes a valued service provider, and credibility starts to emerge on both sides. Sales understands that the revenue engine requires both an effective marketing engine, as well as an effective sales engine. Eventually, Marketing and Sales become trusted partners that collaborate closely on all fronts and never want to navigate challenges alone. The best compliment you'll ever get from Sales is when they don't want to continue the discussion without you or a member of your marketing team present. Believe it or not, it does happen and it's a wonderful thing when it does.

Let's talk about systems and technology. Ask Sales what they think of Marketing's usage of automation technologies. Ask your team to tell you about Sales' current usage of technology such as your customer relationship management (CRM) platform. Ask both groups how well Marketing & Sales' technologies talk to each other? How well do they think these tools are integrated? Furthermore, ask both how well they think your organization is managing its data? How do we manage data as an organization? As a prospect, is data kept in a separate database from customer data? Why? Is it largely inaccurate or incomplete? Can I use that data to effectively call on a customer and understand all that they've interacted with before my call? How can I use that data to predict or identify those that are in an active buying cycle? While it might be surprising to hear that Sales would have an opinion about Marketing's use of technology, sales reps today are aware of technology because they are educated consumers themselves. Amazon has trained us all on the experiences we should expect from companies. Sales may complain about the state of your website, or the personalization you're using in your email blasts or inability to quickly respond to someone who engages with your company on social media profiles. On the flip side, Marketing also has a point of view on how Sales is using CRM, whether they're widely and consistently using it, whether they're held accountable for entering opportunities before they're closed or associated contacts with their opportunities. Both groups will certainly use the health of your database as an indication of how well the other group is using their technology. For example, you might hear that it takes Marketing three weeks to upload leads from webinars. They may not sit there and say that clearly there's a lack of integration between the technologies that Marketing uses and Sales use, but they sure as heck know that it took three weeks to get a lead. Understanding how Marketing and Sales team members view your organization's use of technology and data can help you establish priorities and gain advocacy for additional investment to solve gaps.

Messaging and materials are the last drivers to ask about. How is marketing and sales collateral developed and used today? And how aligned is our message in the market? Sales might say, "Hey, the collateral from Marketing is often thrown away. Instead, we develop our own materials because we have a better understanding of what will resonate with the buyer." On the flip side of that, they might share the two functions, collaborate on all the marketing materials and the collateral they have is easy to find. Sales reps might feel that it is easy to customize or personalize content for buyers, and that the content effectively supports their selling conversations. Marketing might know which assets are used Sales, which are consumed by the prospect and how those assets are impacting opportunities and sales wins.

Finally, how aligned is your messaging in the market? For immature organizations, Sales' messaging is different from the messaging developed by Marketing. Sales is aware of Marketing's messaging strategy but choose to use different messages because they believe that marketing's messages do not resonate with customers. As organizations mature, Sales begins to integrate marketing and brand messages into their sales discussions until there is a true partnership in the development and on-going refinement of messaging.

When you ask the same survey questions of both Marketing and Sales, you will get a crystal-clear picture of where you are aligned and where your greatest opportunities for improvement are.

Sales & Marketing Alignment Criteria	Marketing	Sales
Organizational Relationships	3.0	1.7
Metrics & Value-Measurement	3.2	1.6
Demand Generation & Demand Waterfall Management	3.0	2.3
Company Culture	2.0	1.8
Systems & Technology	3.5	2.3
Messaging & Materials	4.5	1.0
Weighted Sales & Marketing Alignment Score (out of 100)	62.22	36.05

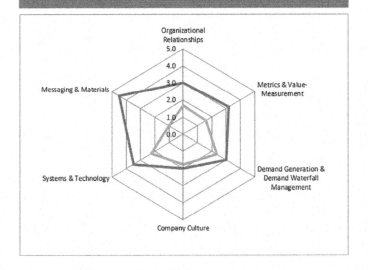

Sales & Marketing Alignment Guage

For example, you might uncover that you're closely aligned on a number of these drivers, whether it's company culture and the way you generate demand but you're misaligned on metrics & value measurement, or the messaging and materials that are being developed and used in the market. There are two key benefits of using this mirrored survey approach, one, you quickly identify the sources of conflict between Marketing and Sales, and, two, you identify the challenges you both believe should be addressed. What's better? You can repeat this survey every quarter or every year and see how the relationship is improving and strengthening across these key drivers.

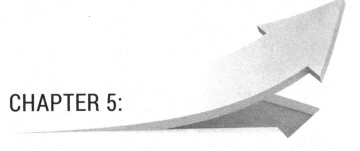

CHAPTER 5:

Get Your Change Levers in Order to Maximize Impact

As a marketing leader, you know that there are several changes needed to build a revenue engine capable of enabling you to become a business driver for your organization. Through two decades of advising marketing leaders and wrestling with the same challenges myself, there always comes a moment where you feel like there are too many things that need to change in order to transform from an activities-based support function to a revenue engine capable of driving the business. For many marketers, this moment results in a crisis of confidence. You find yourself in a valley of doubt because you simply don't know where to start or in which order to change things to deliver maximum, positive business impact.

To jumpstart your stalled demand engine and help your company return to revenue growth, you'll need to improve your sales and marketing processes. I refer to these sales and marketing processes as change levers because with a small amount of change you'll experience an exponential improvement in revenue performance. For each one of the change levers, there are stages of process maturity your organization can advance through. Depending on your organizational priorities, your current capabilities and how much time and money you have to invest, your job will be to either systematically mature across the stages for each one of these change levers or leapfrog the stages of maturity to get to the desired state faster.

This chapter provides you with a self-assessment tool that will help you quickly identify which change levers need to be pulled and which order to pull them in to successfully drive the kind of transformative change your business needs. I have tested and refined this tool over the last decade, having used it many times for client organizations. I've also effectively used it myself as a marketing leader for two different global organizations.

Before we complete the self-assessment, let's take a moment to talk about the elephant in the room. The change elephant, if you will. If you want to jump-start your demand engine and help your organization return to revenue growth, you will be driving transformational change that can feel overwhelming at times. Whenever it was clear that one of my team members was feeling overwhelmed and stuck, I'd ask them a seemingly unrelated, silly question to help them get past the feeling of being overwhelmed and into action. "How do you eat an elephant?" Initially, they'd just wait for me to explain the strange question and tell them the answer. And my answer was always "A bite at a time." Over time, I noticed they started coaching themselves and each other by asking that silly, random question to keep moving forward. One day I returned from lunch to find this photo on my office wall.

Apparently, my team felt that my office walls were too empty and thought this was a perfect way to use the space to provide a consistent reminder to all of my visitors that might be feeling overwhelmed and stuck.

While I'd love to take credit for this simple yet effective strategy, it was the brainchild of Desmond Tutu, a Nobel Prize Laureate. Desmond felt that everything in life that seems daunting, overwhelming, and even impossible can be accomplished gradually by taking on just a little at a time.

Just like we wouldn't try to eat an elephant all at one time, we aren't going to change everything at one time. One bite at a time. One change at a time. Levers are the key drivers of any effective revenue engine. To identify and prioritize the changes that will have the greatest impact, you'll evaluate six key drivers for profitable revenue generation:

1. Marketing's role in revenue generation
2. Technology and infrastructure
3. Data management
4. Lead management processes
5. Programs
6. Measurement and reporting

As we review each driver, I'll describe the state of that process in four maturity levels with level 1 being immature and level 4 being advanced.

Marketing's role in revenue generation. What is marketing's role in revenue generation today? For level one maturity, marketing is responsible for the completion of activities, things like email sends, events, logistics, support, collateral development. Level two, you're responsible for generating hand-raisers, initial inquiries. Level three, you're responsible for generating marketing qualified leads. Level four, you have accepted responsibility for marketing-sourced and influenced revenue goals. You've gone on the hook for a number.

What are your key performance metrics? How is your success measured consistent with your role in the organization? Level one marketers don't have success metrics outside the execution of marketing activities. Level two marketers are measured by the number of inquiries generated. Level three marketers are measured by meeting MQL volume quantity as well as sales acceptance rate of leads. Level four marketers are measured by sourced or influenced revenues both in terms of dollars and percentage of revenues.

What is Marketing's role in sales enablement? Level one marketers do not invest in sales enablement. Level two marketers play some role in sales enablement but usually limited to sales asset management. Level three marketers play a significant role in sales enablement — where in addition to sales assets you're also enabling white space analysis, go to market planning, territory playbooks, and list acquisition for sales outreach. Level four marketers provide full enablement support, with market and buyer intelligence, sales campaigns in a box with customizable email templates, and sales playbooks on how to effectively manage each selling scenario.

Level one marketers don't own any responsibility for creating demand and how it gets converted. Level four marketers say, "Look, I'm on the hook for making sure that the demand we create converts at the greatest possible chances ever. Here's everything you need to know about the market and the buyer. Here are the tools you need to reach out to them. And oh, by the way, these are the tools that will help to improve your efficiency and effectiveness, so you maximize precious selling time."

Technology and infrastructure. While we've already talked about this as part of the alignment perception survey, this is a factual assessment of how Marketing is using automation and technology. Level one marketers use no marketing technology at all. If you're reading this book, odds are you've already invested in marketing automation. But are you using it to its full potential? Level two marketers may have invested in marketing automation technology but are still treating it like a batch and blast email engine. Consequently, level two marketers are surely wasting some of the demand they're creating because they're not using functionality like multidimensional lead scoring. Level three marketers might have marketing automation and using some of its advanced functionality, but it's not integrated with anything else so there's a lot of manual data manipulation and/or transferring of data between marketing automation and CRM platforms. Level four marketers are not only fully leveraging the power of marketing automation, but the technologies are integrated so there is a holistic 360-degree view of the customer.

Speaking of customers, how does your organization use its CRM platform? (If you don't have a CRM, that's probably the most urgent need for the organization.) Level one organizations don't have CRM implemented, depending on disparate excel worksheets to manage the business. Level two organizations have CRM implemented, but sales reps only use it to report on what's necessary to get paid. They are reluctant users. Level three organizations have it and the organization struggles with using it for pre sales-qualified opportunity stage leads. Level four organizations are CRM innovators using CRM for full process automation, full visibility throughout the marketing and sales pipeline, high degree of confidence and reports.

Data management. What is the current state of your database? Level one marketers keep their data in spreadsheets, usually on employees' laptops or shared folders in the cloud. Level two marketers often have multiple databases. Level three marketers have one centralized database that has flat data structures not conducive for account-based marketing and sales strategies. Level four marketers have a centralized marketing database with a rich data structure that enables their organization to ensure that every interaction with your brand builds on where the last interaction left off.

As for the state of the records within your database, does your organization have any sort of data governance in place today? How do you make sure records are up to date? Do you have an ongoing data cleansing and enrichment tool to make sure that the fields themselves on the records are complete, but that they also support highly targeted segmentation by both Marketing and Sales? For example, if you were to design and execute a campaign targeting a marketing leader, would you be able to segment your data based on not only who they are and their organization, but also the challenge that they're facing as demonstrated by their buying behavior? If you trust that your team would be able to design and execute that campaign based on your current data, then you have an accurate, complete, and marketable database. If you're not sure, here are the stages of maturity. Level one marketers have no idea what condition their data is in. Level two marketers have limited to no governance and often find themselves struggling with old records maintained in the database because Sales' feels it's more important to maintain historical records than keeping the database free of dirty data. As an example, I once argued with a sales leader about whether to keep deceased people in the database. His argument was that it helped sales reps understand if we had ever sold to someone within an organization. My argument was that we were damaging our brand by marketing to people that had died. While you might think I am kidding about this, it was real. We had been marketing to people that had died. How did I know that? We had received a phone call from an executive assistant asking us to please stop sending emails and direct mail to him. It was understandably upsetting. Level three marketers have on-going data cleansing and standardization but completeness in key fields does not support highly targeted segmentation. Level four marketers benefit from a high degree of accuracy and completeness to support advanced segmentation needs.

Lead management. Since lead definition is the single greatest rallying point between Marketing and Sales in a B2B organization, do you have a universally accepted and documented definition of a lead with Sales? You either do or you don't. Somewhere in the middle is the belief that Marketing thinks they know what that definition is, but it's not proven and documented with Sales.

How are inbound inquiries managed today? Level one marketers do not capture inquiries in a centralized database. They have significantly broken response channels. Level two marketers allow inbound inquiries to flow directly to Sales with little to no screening prior to sending. Level three marketers use simple lead scoring to screen out junk leads or a lead ranking model that triggers when to send inquiries to a tele-qualification function versus a field sales rep. Finally, level four marketers leverage a multi-dimensional lead scoring model that triages leads based on their role, company and the significance, frequency, and recency of their activities. They may also score leads based on buying intent data gathered from 3rd party sources. While it sounds complex, technology has advanced to the degree that it doesn't take a rocket scientist to help you leverage your data to identify, screen, qualify and handle leads based on their fit and sales-readiness.

Now, let's talk about your organization's sales coverage model. For B2B organizations that are selling complex or highly technical solutions that are considered purchases, inevitably someone must talk to the lead to qualify needs and confirm sales-readiness. If that's true and your organization has set up a tele-qualification function either internally or externally with an agency partner, you must make sure that every stage of the lead lifecycle is supported organizationally—no leads are left behind through the process. For some organizations, marketing owns the tele-qualification as part of that lead handling process. In others, that tele-qualification function falls entirely within the sales organization or sits in between as an outsourced function that sits between Marketing and Sales. The important takeaway here is that you have a clearly defined process that not only documents where the key hand-offs are, but also what is expected of lead recipients when a lead is received. Make sure everyone understands how best to advance the lead towards a sale as quickly as possible.

Finally, what is your current turnaround time on from initial hand raising or engagement to sales rep follow-up? Level one marketers have no idea how long it takes. Level two marketers know what the turnaround time is but it takes weeks or months. Level three marketers know what it is and it's within a couple of days. While there's some room for optimization, the world's not on fire. Level four marketers can measure lead response time in hours and minutes, and it's fully optimized. They are truly engaging in their buyer's moment of interest.

Programs. How do you create demand in the market? How are marketing messages planned and executed? Level one marketers either suffer from occasional communications with no segmentation and no sense of urgency. Level two marketers find that everything is a time sensitive random act of marketing with little to no segmentation. Level three marketers are consistent in their communications but it's frequently one size fits all Level four marketers are highly targeted and personalized in their communications. They're effectively making sure that every message builds on where the lead's last interaction with the brand left off.

How are your programs currently implemented? What areas of the lead life cycle are they focused on? Level one marketers are only focused on generating a net new lead but have zero programs intended to nurture leads until they are qualified and sales ready. Level two marketers have some balance between generating that net new lead and nurturing until they're sales ready. Level three marketers have programs focused on every stage of the buying journey, working in concert with whatever Sales may or may not be doing. Level four marketers also have recycling and save programs intended to save stalled or disqualified leads.

Do you have the needed content to fuel your programs? Does your existing library of content support every stage of that lead lifecycle or buyer's journey to be an enabler or accelerator of the purchasing decision? Level one marketers have little to no content that can be leveraged for marketing programs beyond generating a net new lead. Level two marketers have some gaps in content that make nurturing programs limited across channels. Level three has extensive content coverage for nurturing but has not repurposed the content into different forms (video, blog post, infographic, etc.) that can be leveraged across different platforms or they lack content that can be used to re-engage stalled leads. Level four marketers have strong content coverage in the context of a buyer persona that answers all their key questions across their decision-making process and is available in different forms on different platforms.

Measurement and reporting. How do you prove marketing's performance and impact? What level of marketing measurement are you able to use to achieve with your current tools? Level one marketers are limited to the status of activities: planned and completed. Level two marketers struggle with ad hoc, manual reporting on the results of activities and performance against budget. They're taking data from multiple databases and manually aggregating that data to answer a question. Level three marketers have standard dashboards. They're consistently updated, but they are limited to the moment where Marketing sends leads over to Sales. Level four marketers enjoy end-to-end visibility with real time aggregated reporting across the different levels of measurement from the database health, the effective execution of planned activities, the immediate results of those activities, pipeline and revenue impact with full revenue attribution across marketing investments.

Can a business leader diagnose your marketing and sales pipelines to identify potential challenges and/or opportunities? Do you have an integrated view of the marketing and sales pipeline? Level one marketers are not aware that there is such a thing as an integrated view of the marketing and sales pipeline, much less able to report on it or diagnose it. Level two marketers know what an integrated view of the marketing and sales pipeline looks like but to deliver that view, there is a tremendous amount of manual reporting through spreadsheets and PowerPoints. Level three marketers have automated reports, but low adoption of CRM means that the closed loop, end-to-end visibility is still challenged. If Sales isn't actively updating what's happening to opportunities that have converted from leads, your reporting can only go so far. Level four marketers have automated, near-real time, end-to-end visibility of how demand flows through your organization and turns into revenue across all stages, the demand waterfall. That's the holy grail for marketers that want to be viewed as business drivers for their organization.

When you assess your Sales & Marketing process maturity across these key drivers of revenue generation using this framework, it should be very easy to identify which change levers you need to pull. As for the order of operations, start first by improving the areas where you are at a maturity level of one or two ratings. This will eliminate the potential of any wasted demand. From there, work to gain organizational acceptance for elevating marketing's role in revenue generation to going on the hook for a revenue number with a sourced or influenced revenue goal. Once you have buy-in and support, quickly address the gaps in your technology, data and reporting then fuel the engine by expanding your programs.

When I first started as a marketing leader for a global management consulting firm years ago, we uncovered that all our inbound inquiries flowed directly to Sales without any sort of screening and that the average lead turnaround time was 37 days! It was painfully obvious that lead management processes had to be the first lever to pull. Once we fixed the big leaks in our lead management processes, we turned our attention to the next logical steps, gaining support for establishing an integrated view of the marketing and sales pipeline, a universally accepted definition of a lead and an executed mutual service level agreement that detailed roles and responsibilities across the entire lead lifecycle. We then used that service level agreement to engage in the conversation with IT about technology and data requirements needed to deliver on the service level agreement and improve the way the entire organization created and managed leads through to revenue. Once you understand how each of the levers work, there is a natural order to pull them in.

Transforming Marketing into a revenue engine is not as hard as it sounds if you think logically. For example, you can't establish lead scoring models to identify and qualify potential leads if you don't obtain Sales' definition of what a qualified, sales-ready lead looks like. The lead scoring model won't work if you don't have accurate, complete data in the fields that the lead scoring model relies upon. There's no sense in reporting on an integrated view of the Marketing and Sales pipeline if the organization doesn't understand the linkage between the two pipelines or how marketing performance can influence revenue forecasts.

Assess your current process maturity, make decisions on what you'll improve, establish an order or operations, give your team a clear roadmap for the next right steps and support them with clear operating philosophies.

Naeem Callaway also said "Sometimes the smallest step in the right direction can be the biggest step of your life." What is your next right step to advance your capabilities from the current state to the desired future state?

THE REVENUE
RAMP

Phase 2: **Align**

Aligning your
organization on key drivers
of revenue growth.

CHAPTER 6:

Make it Official

The ability of your organization to align the activities of Marketing and Sales is one of the most impactful drivers of revenue performance and competitive advantage. In fact, alignment can mean the difference between business growth and decline:

- Forrester found that business-to-business organizations with tightly aligned marketing and sales operations organization achieves 19% faster revenue growth and 15% higher profitability than misaligned organizations.[10]
- Aberdeen Group found that highly aligned organizations achieved an average of 32% year-over-year

---

[10] Forrester (2019) Introducing the Sirius7™: Seven Elements to Align in Your Revenue Engine. Retrieved from: https://go.forrester.com/blogs/how-to-align-revenue-engine/

revenue growth—while their less aligned competitors saw a 7% decrease in revenue.[11]

- MarketingProfs found that organizations with tightly aligned sales and marketing functions experience 36% higher customer retention rates and 38% higher sales win rates.[12]

The root causes of misalignment include unclear linkage between the Marketing and Sales pipelines, lead definitions and roles and responsibilities along the lead lifecycle. All of which can be solved with development and execution of a two-way service level agreement between Marketing and Sales that establishes an integrated view of the revenue pipeline, defines lead requirements and outlines roles and responsibilities across the lead lifecycle.

First, let's address the one thing that can either help or hinder your ability to improve Sales' perception of Marketing and their willingness to partner with you: the lack of clear linkage between the marketing and sales pipelines. As a result of unclear linkage between the marketing and sales pipelines business leaders do not fully understand the cause-effect between marketing efforts and revenue. This is often the root cause of Marketing being viewed by Finance as a cost center. Businesses often invest anywhere

---

[11] Houpis, C. (2010) Sales and Marketing Alignment: Collaboration + Cooperation + Peak Performance. Aberdeen Group. Retrieved from: https://www.dnb.com/content/dam/english/dnb-solutions/sales-and-marketing/aberdeen_report_sales_and_marketing_alignment_2010_09.pdf

[12] Handley, A. (2016) 2016 B2B Content Marketing Benchmarks, Budgets, and Trends. MarketingProfs. Retrieved from: https://www.marketingprofs.com/charts/2015/28555/2016-b2b-content-marketing-benchmarks-budgets-and-trends

from 2-6% of revenue in Marketing and yet don't see evidence of how that directly sources or influences revenue. If you want to be viewed as a business driver, you will have to establish one unified view of the marketing and sales pipeline then prove how the efforts and investments of one impacts the other.

Having used the Sales & Marketing Alignment Perception Survey to create awareness for the benefits of linking the marketing and sales pipelines, you can now get to work on establishing an integrated view of the marketing and sales pipeline. If you're already operating with an integrated view of the marketing and sales pipeline, you may still need to make some changes if the pipeline is too simplistic to support the needs of your organization. Here is what an overly simplistic view of the pipeline looks like:

This simplistic view of the integrated marketing and sales pipeline prevents any sort of feedback mechanism on the quality of the leads that Marketing has generated. It does not account for demand that is sourced outside of Marketing which then creates situations where Sales and Marketing fight over who has sourced the lead. It also doesn't acknowledge the role of tele-qualification in the demand creation and lead qualification processes and leads to under-resourcing of the tele-qualification function as it's difficult to manage and measure the team's productivity. The simplified view basically assumes that we're able to glean the qualification and sales readiness without ever talking to the lead on the phone. For B2B organizations selling highly technical products or complex solutions, the phone is often required to validate needs and verify sales-readiness.

Furthermore, the simplistic view of the pipeline only allows for forward progression because it doesn't enable any sort of feedback mechanisms or formal processes to return leads to Marketing for additional cultivation. This prevents the execution of long-term strategies such as lead nurturing, recycling of stalled leads, and winning back lost leads and opportunities.

Finally, this simplistic view of the pipeline doesn't support route-around rules or customization to meet the unique requirements of different business units, regions, accounts, product offerings, etc. For example, if your organization has a strategic or key account, Marketing will not be able to route around any inbound lead from a strategic account to put it right in the hands of the account team. All leads will be treated equally following the same pre-defined qualification process established for all other leads. While a simplistic integrated view of the marketing and sales pipelines are better than treating them separately, organizations quickly experience challenges as their marketing and sales processes mature.

Recognizing the limitations of the simplistic view of the integrated marketing and sales pipeline in 2012, Sirius Decisions published an advanced view of the integrated revenue pipeline called the SiriusDecisions Rearchitected Demand Waterfall®. This modular framework provides Marketing and Sales with the tools needed to optimize how demand is created and managed through to revenue. It enables you to account for demand that is sourced outside of marketing. It openly acknowledges the role of tele-qualification in the lead management process. It enables advanced nurturing strategies like lead recycling. It allows for route-around rules based on exceptions. It enables organizations to customize the pipeline based on market or region-specific strategies. It is the most flexible yet comprehensive view of the integrated demand and revenue pipeline for a company. Adopting this universally accepted framework makes it easier for you to find industry-specific benchmark data to assess your organization's performance after implementation. This can be very helpful in establishing reasonable goals in absence of historical data.

That said, it doesn't matter whether you adopt Sirius Decisions Rearchitected Demand Waterfall® as-is, customize it to more closely align to your sales coverage model or create an entirely new version of an integrated marketing and sales pipeline for your organization. What matters most is that Marketing and Sales are aligned on one integrated view of the marketing and sales pipeline, agreeing to have a clearly defined stage for each key stage of the lead management process with accept/reject functionality at key hand-offs and agreement on how those stages are defined, tracked and measured.

One additional thing to note is that the sales qualified opportunity stage within the demand waterfall does not replace all standard opportunity stages that you have in your CRM. Opportunity stages should nestle nicely as sub-stages of the sales qualified opportunity demand waterfall stage.

Always remember, most Marketing and Sales mis-alignment stems from people talking about the same thing but using different terminology. This is especially true when talking about the marketing and sales pipeline stages as well as the definition of a lead and how leads flow through the pipeline. According to CSO insights, less than 44% of companies have a formally agreed upon definition of a qualified lead between Sales and Marketing. Given that Sales and Marketing alignment hinges on what a lead is or isn't, this chapter will show you how to gain universal acceptance for the definition of a qualified, sales-ready lead.

What exactly IS a lead? Throughout my career, I've asked hundreds of marketers and sales executives to answer this simple question. In nearly all cases, the definition of a lead varies greatly between the two functions of the same company.

It is helpful to think of a lead as a person that has engaged with some sort of offer and meets at least basic qualification criteria. That lead can be a net new person/record coming into your database, or an existing person/record in your database that has expressed renewed interest. There are a variety of lead stages that align with where the lead is in their buyers' journey / decision making process. Marketing and Sales should align on when that lead should be viewed as qualified and "sales-ready"—that is, worthy of Sales' pursuit. In a perfect world, that moment will closely align with where the buyer believes the sales rep adds value to the buying / decision making process.

Commonly used lead criteria to define whether a lead is qualified and sales-ready includes: is it the right organization where we can win? Is it the right contact in the organization (function and organization level) that either owns or influences the buying decision? Is there a defined need or problem that we can solve? Have they demonstrated the right behaviors, either through the significance, frequency or recency of activity that indicate they are in an active buying process? Have you been able to either interpret an implied need, or has the lead themselves explicitly stated their need? Have you identified or established that they have a budget and a purchasing decision timeline through your interactions? If you have, does that decision timeline fall within what would be an acceptable timeline for Sales to start working the lead?

Now that we have established an integrated view of the marketing and sales pipeline that supports the needs of the organization, it's time to clearly define what a qualified and sales-ready lead looks like for Sales.

Before we get started, it's important to note that there are three undisputed truths about leads:

1. **The definition of a qualified, sales-ready lead is whatever Sales says it is.**
2. **Unlike humans, all leads are not created equal.**
3. **Lead pursuit time to follow up is the greatest driver of conversion.**

Accelerating profitable revenue growth requires your company to decide what you won't waste precious selling time on so you can quickly pursue the right opportunities you can and want to win.

Clearly defining what a qualified, sales-ready lead looks like requires bringing the right people from the Sales organization together to get aligned on the answer to a clear set of questions. These answers will become the definition of a qualified, sales-ready lead. As an experienced marketer, you may already know the answers to the questions, but the goal is to let Sales know that you listened to them as they describe what is worth their time to pursue.

Let's get into the nitty gritty details of the workshop. You'll look to schedule a three-hour workshop and invite at least one to three representatives from each level of the sales organization. The desired group size is 14-20 representatives as you'll want adequate representation from the different levels of sales organization including sales operations. Here's an example of the proposed audience makeup:

- Vice President (1)
- Sales Directors (1 to 2)
- Regional Sales Managers (2 to 3)
- Account Managers / Field Sales Representatives (5 to 6)
- Inside Sales Manager (1 to 2)
- Inside Sales Specialists (3 to 5)
- Sales Operations Leader (1)

Within the group, you will want a mix of credible high performers and include both long tenured sales reps as well as those that are new to the organization—especially if you're experiencing a shift in your go-to-market strategy. Finally, it is good to invite your key marketers as well as key members from IT that need to understand business requirements for how leads will be managed in the desired future state. To be clear, Marketing and IT will be observers, not active participants. This workshop is intended for Marketing to learn what Sales thinks is worthy of their selling time and what they need to effectively convert leads.

Now that we understand who should attend the session, here is an overview of the most common criteria that you'll use to establish a lead definition for your organization:

- Right Organization
- Right Person
- Right Activity
  - o Significance of Activity
  - o Frequency of Activity
  - o Recency of Activity
- Right Need
  - o Implied Need
  - o Explicitly Stated Need
- Established Budget
- Validated Decision Timeline

To determine what is the right organization for Sales to pursue, ask these questions: How would you describe your ideal customer organization? Is there such a thing as an organization that is too small? Is there such a thing as an organization being too large? For example, does your value proposition and ability to win change based on the size of the company? Does the size of the company complicate the purchasing process? Is geography important? Would you pursue an international lead? If you do, are you pursuing it with a direct sales rep or do we need to think about channel partners, and how we make sure that channel partners receive leads and know what to do with them? And how do we close the feedback loop with leads distributed to partners, knowing that they're not internal employees working within our systems?

To determine if the lead is the right person to pursue, ask these questions: How many buying influencers are involved in the buying committee? Are there any entry points that make it harder to close a profitable sale like purchasing and procurement as an example? To guide this part of the discussion, provide a list of potential functional groups and position levels to make it easy for the group to quickly evaluate which people do/don't make sense for your organization to pursue. Functional groupings are employees that share similar areas of expertise, doing similar work, solving similar challenges and aligned to common goals. Position level indicates where the position falls within the organization's hierarchy as an indicator of purchasing authority and influence.

If you're selling a complex product or service, do we need to think about leads in terms of the opportunities, or do we think about a lead in the context of an individual person? For one organization, we had identified 37 engaged buying influencers from the same healthcare provider. This was the committee in charge of finding a solution to one business problem. For mature organizations, the 37 engaged people represented one sales lead, not 37 leads.

To understand which activities drive the right behaviors that indicate sales-readiness, try to uncover which behaviors Sales deem worthy of pursuing. Ask these "what if" questions (in this specific order):

- Person submits a Contact Me, Demo Request, Software Trial Request or Submit-RFP Website Form?
- Person subscribes for additional content/insights/ communications?
- Person attends a webinar?
- Person registers for but doesn't attend the webinar?
- Person watches a pre-recorded webinar?
- Person attends a speaking session at a 3rd party event?
- Person attends a large, casual networking event?
- Person visits your booth at an exhibition/trade show?
- Person completes an online poll, self-assessment tool or a return-on-investment (ROI) or total cost of ownership (TCO) calculator on your website?
- Person download a simple piece of content like a product brochure?
- Person visits our website but did not complete a webform asking to be contacted?
- Person opens or clicks on an email but did not complete a webform asking to be contacted?
- Organization or person is identified by an intent monitoring or predictive analytics service as actively seeking a product / service or solution but has not yet engaged with your organization?

If you ask these questions in this order, the group will quickly realize that not every lead is qualified, sales-ready—every lead is not created equal. By the time you get to website visits and email clicks, you'll be hearing a chorus of nos. If not, you'll want to pause and share what those quantities look like and how more is not always better. Sending everything over often leads to slower turnaround times on truly qualified, sales-ready leads simply because there's only so much time in the day to pursue leads. For example, one of the companies I worked at attracted 100K unique visitors to our website per month and because of advanced technologies we were able to determine which companies they were. There's way too much to think about pursuing those leads prematurely. If all else fails and you still cannot convince the group that pursuing some of these would be premature, ask them how they'd feel if a company's sales rep called them if they completed the same action. Does a follow up phone call after opening but not clicking through an email make sense? Odds are they'll view that as too aggressive.

Now that you know the right company, right person and right activity requirements, you'll need to get alignment on identified needs, established budget and decision timing. For a lead to be deemed as qualified, does a specific need, concern, area of interest, or defined project need to be implied or explicitly stated? Are there any expressed needs that are less-than-desirable fit for your solution; not worth pursuing? Does Sales feel like Marketing must confirm that there is a budget already established for the solution before passing the lead on for follow up? If so, you are more than likely waiting too long to pursue leads as most organizations either don't have or don't communicate defined budgets before engaging with Sales. As for decision timing, is 90 days too late? Too soon? How about 6 months? One full year? 18 months? Sales will often say that it's never too soon but there's a lot of data that shows if a lead isn't going to convert to a qualified opportunity that has the potential to convert within 1-2 quarters it will get dropped, mishandled or ignored altogether due to the quarterly pressure Sales is under.

Finally, this is your opportunity to ask Sales what information they require to effectively pursue leads. Make it a point to differentiate between what is required and what would be helpful information to support an effective selling conversation.

Required information looks like:

- **Contact name**
- **Contact phone number**
- **Contact email address**
- **Organization name**
- **Organization address (Zip/Postal Code, or City + State/Province, Country)**
- **At least one product, software, solution OR business application of interest implied through activity or expressly stated in a web form**
- **Campaign and lead source details**

Helpful information looks like:

- **Budget**
- **Decision timeline**
- **Desired follow up time for sales appointment**
- **A link into CRM to view related, active sales opportunities**

Now that you understand what constitutes a qualified, sales-ready lead, you must clearly define who does what along the lead lifecycle to eliminate wasted opportunities and maximize lead conversion. Many B2B organizations have some sort of tele-qualification, inside sales, or business development team that is responsible for further qualifying a lead using the phone or website chat functionality. To make sure I provide you with enough guidance on how to navigate this discussion, I'll assume you have the three core functions responsible for generating, qualifying, and converting leads into opportunities and sales: Marketing, Inside Sales, and Field Sales. With that assumption, I'll provide you with a series of questions that you can take your group through. If you only have Marketing and Sales, you can simplify this list of questions to account for key hand-offs between just two versus three functions.

Here's the list of questions:

- How many hours does Marketing have to pass on leads to sales once the lead has crossed the agreed-upon requirement threshold?
- How do we know who to assign the lead to within the tele-qualification/inside sales/business development team? (no general queues)
- A tele-qualification/inside sales/business development rep must accept or reject a lead from marketing within how many minutes or hours of receipt?
- How many weeks do we allow the tele-qualification/inside sales/business development rep to work that lead before it must be promoted or disqualified?

- Under what special circumstances may Marketing by-pass tele-qualification/inside sales/business development to deliver leads directly to Sales (account managers)?
- In the case of a route-around, how will Marketing know who to route the lead to?
- If a lead is routed around the tele-qualification/inside sales/business development team, what will Sales promise to do with the lead, and in what timeframe?
- What are the consequences for those who fail to act on fast-track leads?
- How should leads be delivered from tele-qualification/inside sales/business development to the Sales team?
- Must an appointment be scheduled for the sales rep? Does the tele-qualification/inside sales/business development rep attend that call for a warm handoff?
- How much time do you allocate for the sales rep to work that lead before it must be converted or disqualified?
- If a lead has not been converted or disqualified within the prescribed time frame, can the Marketing or tele-qualification/inside sales/business development organization pull it back?
- What are the legitimate reasons a tele-qualification/inside sales/business development rep can reject a lead?
- What are the valid disqualification reasons that would send a lead from tele-qualification/inside sales/business development back to Marketing?

- What should Marketing's response be, if any, to rejected leads? Do those actions vary by rejection reason?
- What is Marketing's responsibility for disqualified leads? Should nurture streams be defined for any specific disqualification reasons?
- If a lead has not been promoted or disqualified within the prescribed time frame, can Marketing pull it back? If not, why not?
- What is the process for requesting an extension for leads that have not been promoted or disqualified?
- What are Marketing and Inside Sales teams' responsibilities in supporting sales reps that have stalled leads?

Leads are generated from many sources, Google search, online advertising, traditional advertising, syndicated content with industry trade publications, email blasts, and all forms of events. The challenge, though, is that we don't know exactly what sales executives would consider worthy of their selling time. We don't know exactly what information they need to effectively pursue those leads. We don't know who's best positioned to manage leads at the different stages of the lead life-cycle. We don't know if lead recipients know how best to manage leads. We make lots of assumptions along the way in terms of what it takes to effectively convert leads into opportunities and close sales. These underlying assumptions lead to misalignment and significant wasted demand. While validating or correcting assumptions is a lot of work, it is worth it.

Translating the findings from the lead definition workshop into an executable service level agreement is straightforward. First, you'll consolidate all the answers to the questions you posed during the workshop into a cohesive word document. The document should include a clear definition of what a qualified sales-ready lead looks like, the key hand-offs across the lead lifecycle in the context of your integrated view of the marketing and sales pipeline along as well as a description for who does what at every stage of that lead lifecycle. Additionally, you should include how compliance with the mutual SLA will be measured and how the SLA will be continuously maintained and optimized.

When you're ready, submit a draft document to the workshop participants for feedback and proposed edits. Incorporate their feedback, sign it then submit the finalized version to the head of Sales for signature. The signature adds credibility to the process and document, signaling to everyone that Marketing and Sales leaders are aligned on the requirements outlined, and that everyone is going to be held accountable for complying with what is documented.

Implementing your newly executed SLA will more than likely require changes to your marketing automation or CRM platforms to effectively enable the new lead management workflow. For some organizations, changes might include the development of a lead scoring model, improving data integration between their marketing automation platform and CRM or replacing general lead queues with a lead assignment engine to ensure direct accountability for lead conversion. Other organizations might have everything they need to identify, qualify and distribute leads with direct accountability but do not have any accept or reject functionality or the appropriate disqualification reasons to support a feedback loop on lead quality and lead recycling programs.

It is important to obtain an approved project plan from IT for the development and testing of the new functionality before you or your team make commitments to Sales about when you'll be able to deliver on the promises outlined in the SLA.

It is okay to have lag between when the SLA is signed and implemented. Use the time in between to prepare a comprehensive communication and training program. Once the enabling infrastructure is tested and ready for go-live, your team can quickly jump into action to prepare the organization for implementation.

Once the SLA has been implemented, remember that you've made a commitment to review the details of this SLA every quarter. The SLA should never be viewed as final and complete. To do this effectively, you'll want to establish a cross-functional lead management council. The lead management council should be the people that attended your lead definition workshop. The lead management council will meet on a quarterly basis to review the SLA along with a sample of the leads that were generated in that quarter. You will update the SLA as you learn more about the market, the buyers, and the strengths of your unified organization. Considering the rapidly evolving market and buyer requirements, the definition of lead should never be stagnant.

Schedule a recurring, hour-long meeting every quarter with your lead management council. During the meeting, review a sample of the leads that were generated in that quarter, leads that have converted both to closed won and closed lost, leads that have stalled and show no activity, and leads that have been rejected right before they were even worked, review them to obtain feedback on the quality of each lead, identify which leads have converted and why.

Solicit this feedback from your lead management council. Are you satisfied with the quality of the leads that were generated? Did you receive enough information along with the leads to convert them into opportunities? For the leads that did turn into closed sales, is there anything unique about those leads that maybe we didn't specifically acknowledge through the lead definition workshop? Any common attributes among the leads that didn't convert? Finally, is the definition of a qualified sales-ready lead defined in the SLA still appropriate?

If yes, great. We'll see you in another quarter. Happy converting. If not, why not? Perhaps lead flow is too constrained and Sales wants to open it up a little bit. If they ask you to loosen up the requirements don't automatically reject them. Remember, the definition of a qualified, sales-ready lead is up to Sales. Here are some examples of requirements that could change:

> *"Hey, we think it's fine to pursue small organizations. Let's lower the organization sizing requirements."*

Or,

> *"Maybe someone that registers for a webinar, but didn't have a chance to attend, we think we want to call on them too instead of only waiting to talk to registered and attended."*

Whether they want to tighten it up or loosen the definitions, just have a thoughtful, honest conversation about what might happen on the other side. If they loosen up lead requirements, they might see an increase in lead quantity but declining conversion rates of leads into opportunities.

Through this review, you'll identify a collection of leads that have been flagged for recycling. These are stalled or lost leads. Review a sample of these and try to uncover if a critical piece of information was missing or if there's an opportunity to re-engage the leads simply by changing the channel of communication or offer strategy.

If a result of these quarterly conversations, and a review of the subset of the data, yields a change, you'll need to make changes to your infrastructure to support it. Often, it's a simple adjustment to a lead scoring model. If you are faced with a go-to market strategy change or a sales coverage model change like the development of a strategic accounts program, you'll need to manage expectations appropriately as the required development work will be more complex. Let Sales know you will partner with IT to scope the work and develop a project plan to make the required changes associated with the new workflow(s). Once you understand the scope of work associated with the proposed changes, you can establish a reasonable timeline for that work to get done.

Do not accommodate changes every week or month. You have committed to Sales that you will have the conversation every quarter, and that will protect you from a never-ending cycle of changes. Demand generation and lead generation are all about momentum. You've got to give the changes a chance to have an impact. If Sales ask for changes midway through a quarter, respond by saying, *"Let's give the new SLA some time to be tested by sufficient lead flow. This will help us make data-driven decisions for optimization."*

Establishing guardrails for review cycles will protect Marketing and IT from always missing expectations associated with moving targets. Now that we've established an integrated view of the revenue pipeline, clearly defined lead requirements, outlined roles and responsibilities across the lead lifecycle, and open the lines of communication, it's time to fix our demand engine and generate some quick wins.

THE REVENUE
RAMP

Phase 3: **Mobilize**

Mobilize Marketing, Sales and IT teams
to quickly fix leaks in your demand
pipeline and secure quick wins.

CHAPTER 7:

Prepare the Organization for Implementation

Congratulations! You now have a clear vision for how your organization will create and convert demand into revenue. To successfully deliver on that vision, Marketing must collaborate with IT to develop the needed infrastructure.

When marketers and tech people work together, the organization wins. Global management consulting firm McKinsey found that companies whose marketing leaders work with their counterparts in Information Technology (IT) to achieve company goals grow their revenues at 10 percent per year—twice as quickly as the average S&P 500 firm.[13] When marketers fail to

---

[13] Boudet, J., Cvetanovski, B., Gregg, B., Heller, J. and Perrey, J. (2019, June) Marketing's moment is now: The C-suite partnership to deliver on growth. McKinsey & Company. Retrieved from: https://www.mckinsey.com/business-functions/marketing-and-sales/our-insights/marketings-moment-is-now-the-c-suite-partnership-to-deliver-on-growth

provide enough details, make technology decisions without the involvement of IT or attempt to re-engineer cross-functional workflows without including IT in the process, they are doomed for failure. Therefore, I recommend including your IT partners from the start, as you cannot successfully drive this type of transformational change without IT's support. This chapter will provide you with an eight-step process to effectively translate what you've developed with Sales into clear functional and technical requirements for your IT partners.

Step One – Create a lead terminology glossary for your new integrated Marketing and Sales pipeline. Compile all of list of all the terminology that Marketing & Sales will need to be aligned on then document a very specific definition for each term, the system from which it originates, any qualifying criteria that must exist, where it fits in your process and what needs to happen to it in order for it to move to a new step in your process. Here are a couple examples of key terms and their definitions:

- **Marketing Qualified Lead:** An inquiry with enough implicit and explicit criteria to meet the threshold for passing to the inside sales or sales or channel organization, depending on routing rules.
- **Lead Routing:** Once a lead has reached an acceptable qualification threshold, it must be passed to an organization for acceptance and processing or rejection with a reason. The lead routing is the set of rules applied to that lead in order to determine

which organization the lead will be routed to. Lead routing rules rely on accurate territory management definitions being maintained.

- **Sales Qualified Opportunity:** A sales concept that represents a sales cycle or buyer's journey once it has reached sales and sales believes there is a reasonable chance to close and win the deal.

- **Conversion Rate:** The number of leads / opportunities that have progressed to a specific stage divided by the total number of leads / opportunities that have been dispositioned from the previous stage. Any demand sitting in the previous stage is not counted against the conversion rate. This method of calculating conversion rates is called "fully progressed," and it is what is used in industry benchmarks.

- **Lead Stage Velocity:** The average amount of time it takes for a lead or opportunity or demand unit to pass from one stage to the next. Only those records that have completed their journey to the next stage are considered when calculating this term. Records that are "in stage" are not used in the calculation, underscoring the importance of dispositioning leads in a timely manner.

Step Two – Translate the executed SLA into a visual depiction of your desired lead management workflow. The details of the lead flow should be fully documented, including all decision points as well as decision criteria. This includes lead inspection and qualification criteria, route-around rules, full disposition of all leads, including re-cycling and desired turn-around times from one lead lifecycle stage to another. For each step in the process, identify the inputs, outputs, processing rules and instructions, supporting systems, and the organizational ownership. If leads are generated by both marketing and sales, you will build a lead flow process map for each scenario—one for marketing sourced leads and another for sales sourced leads. If leads are sourced by marketing, inside sales and field sales, you will develop lead flow process maps for all three.

It's critical to document the lead flow process in a visual format, PowerPoint Smart Graphs, Visio, or Lucidchart work well for this. Here's what you need to visualize in your lead flow process map:

- How does the record come into the system?
- What's the pipeline stage at that point in time?
- Who is responsible for the lead at that stage?
- What actions are required at that stage?
- What is required to advance it to the next stage? (entry criteria)
- What is the desired time at that stage?

Lead flow maps make it easy for all to understand how demand flows through to revenue. Below you will find an example of a lead flow process map:

Illustration of Lead Flow
Marketing to Inside Sales

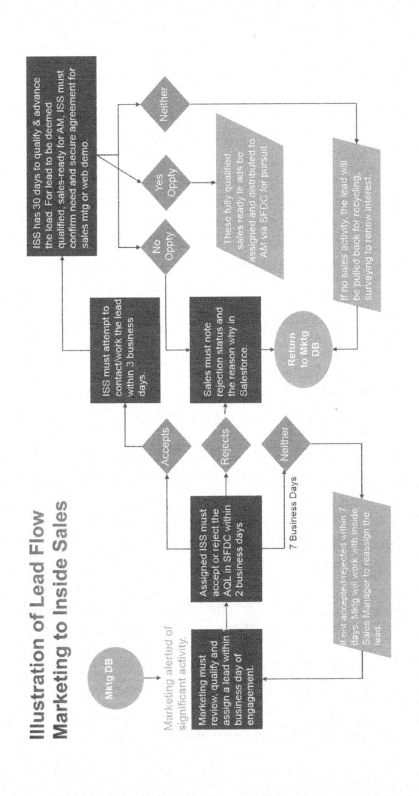

Mktg DB

Marketing alerted of significant activity.

Marketing must review, qualify and assign a lead within business day of engagement.

Assigned ISS must accept or reject the AQL in SFDC within 2 business days

Accepts

Rejects

Neither

7 Business Days

If not accepted/rejected within 7 days, Mktg will work with Inside Sales Manager to reassign the lead.

ISS must attempt to contact/work the lead within 3 business days.

Sales must note rejection status and the reason why in Salesforce.

Return to Mktg DB

ISS has 30 days to qualify & advance the lead. For lead to be deemed qualified, sales-ready for AM, ISS must confirm need and secure agreement for sales mtg or web demo.

No Oppty

Yes Oppty

Neither

These fully qualified, sales ready le ads be assigned and distributed to AM via SFDC for pursuit

If no sales activity, the lead will be pulled back for recycling, surveying to renew interest.

Step Three – Ask a business analyst to translate your lead terminology glossary, executed SLA and lead flow process maps into a technical requirements document and a project plan. If you don't have a business analyst within your team, you might be able to find a business analyst elsewhere within your organizations. Some organizations have business analysts aligned to the IT organization, some have a pool of business analysts centralized within a project management office (PMO) and others either embed the resource within the functions driving strategic initiatives. If there are no available resources, you can outsource this work. Many system implementers, management consulting firms and marketing agencies have business analysts on staff. The technical requirements document should outline requirements for field creation and values, field mapping, lead scoring, lead assignment, lead routing, stage progression and reporting. Once you have a technical requirements document and proposed project plan in hand, your IT partners can start the development of the enabling infrastructure.

Step Four – Since data is the fuel for your demand engine and mass data loads and updates take time, get to work on preparing your database for go-live. Remove duplicate and outdated records from the database. Identify the changes that you need to make to your data model in your different platforms. Are there fields that need to be removed or added? Do you need to change the available field values? What is the plan to populate the new fields that your new workflow will depend on? For example, if you're adding a data field called "demand waterfall stage" and building a business rule that assigns the lead to a sales rep, what happens at go-live when thousands of records don't have a value for that field?

Step Five – Chances are the changing lead requirements will require some changes in your web forms as most of marketing sourced leads flow through websites. In some cases, greater alignment with Sales on required versus nice-to-have information means that fewer form fields will be required and in other cases the available form field values will need to change. A typical website could have hundreds of web forms. Do not wait until the last minute to make the changes and test the integrations.

Step Six—Once this development work is completed, support IT and partner with Sales to help conduct end to end user testing. Recruit volunteers from the sales organization test the new lead management functionality to ensure that it is working as expected to create the best possible, painless rollout experience for the sales reps.

Step Seven—While user testing is underway, dashboards and reports should be built. One set of dashboards and reports should be built for the senior executive team to provide end to end visibility across the entire revenue pipeline. Sales leaders will want the end-to-end reporting for their region or team. Individual sellers will need a dashboard to guide their day-to-day activities. Marketing also needs its reports and dashboards. Remember to address the gaps in data before you build the reports and dashboards. If you forget to address the gaps in your data, the reports will either be empty or unreliable. Don't do all this hard work to establish yourself as a business driver and then have a gap or inaccuracy on a report that undermines your credibility.

Step Eight—After everything has been developed and testing, it is time to train the organization. Conduct foundational training on the new integrated view of the pipeline, the details of the SLA and the process that the organization went through to negotiate that SLA early to create excitement for what's to come. As soon as you're able to record the details of the lead management workflow within your platform(s) and capture screenshots for training materials, you can start training on the actual workflow. Be sure to include training on the available dashboards and reports that will help them manage the business, their overall pipeline and individual leads.

Remember that you cannot successfully drive this type of transformational change without IT's support. Like your Sales peers, your IT partners deserve to be set up for success too. This includes having the necessary details and a reasonable amount of time to develop an enabling infrastructure without creating unnecessary risk or causing disruption to the business. Executing the nine-step process outlined in this chapter will go a long way in ensuring that your vision becomes a reality for your organization.

CHAPTER 8:

Jump Start Your Engine

The most effective way to jumpstart your engine is to recycle the demand you've already created but mismanaged. Recycling stalled and lost demand will enable you to generate enough quick wins to demonstrate business impact, establish credibility and secure the runway that you need for the longer-term transformational change of your function from the doers of things to business drivers.

2020 was extraordinarily difficult for marketers. Businesses were seriously impacted by the pandemic and in many cases, the economic environment completely stalled the marketing engine. For example, many business-to-business organizations relied heavily on trade shows and conferences to generate enough leads to satisfy Sales' growing demand for higher quantities of leads. In March 2020, all in-person events were cancelled or severely delayed. As a marketing leader for a business organization myself, we spent three months trying to negotiate refunds on 65% of our annual marketing spend so that we could reinvest in attracting and engaging our buyers in digital channels.

Unfortunately, many exhibitors were either unwilling or unable to refund payments. The disruption completely exposed our over-dependence on traditional channels. Considering the onslaught of webinars targeting marketing leaders with recommendations on how to manage through the disruption of event cancellations, I'm certain we were not alone. While some were able to quickly pivot, many marketers have since struggled to jumpstart those stalled engines because they spent their time looking for a magic bullet to replace the large number of leads they had expected from the large-scale trade shows.

While there are no such things as magic bullets, there is a source of potential growth that marketers have not looked close enough at. If you're looking to jumpstart your stalled engine and accelerate pipeline growth, look at the leads you've already generated that have either stalled or been lost. Remember, most inquiries won't buy anything within the first 90 days of engaging with your brand, but the overwhelming majority will buy something from your organization in the next year if you continue to show them the love. Before you successfully negotiated your new SLA, you were more than likely prematurely distributing leads.

Chances are the global crisis of Covid-19 caused buyers to delay or cancel projects, especially if budgets were frozen. As economies rebound, buyers might be willing to resume their evaluation of potential solutions or move forward with their purchasing decision. You have an opportunity to re-engage and recycle the stalled or lost leads to generate some quick wins for your organization. Lead recycling programs typically result in recapturing 30-45% of previously stalled or lost leads. Recycling one hundred or even a thousand stalled leads can have a meaningful impact on the pipeline.

Let's first understand what a stalled lead is. In a nutshell, a stalled lead is a sales lead that fails to progress through the pipeline. A lead can stall at any point on the pipeline. However, a sales lead is more likely to stall in the earlier pipeline stages when there is less of a commitment from the prospective buyer. Some leads can stall at the later stages, which can cause the greatest angst for your sales team as there was some commitment and confidence in their ability to close the deal. When the pandemic hit, entire economies came to a screeching halt as businesses shut down. Many purchasing decisions were delayed or cancelled as cash became king. That said, there have always been many reasons leads stalled before the global pandemic disrupted all of us. Sales could have ignored the lead because they didn't believe it was worth their time. They might not have had the right information to effectively pursue the lead. They might have given up after two to three failed attempts at reaching the lead. They might not have had enough time in the day to effectively keep in touch with every lead that delayed projects or had their budgets frozen. Can you imagine how hard it is to stay in front of hundreds or thousands of leads while pressure to close deals today increases? If your job depended on closing deals this month, would you think about constantly staying in touch with a lead whose project was delayed or cancelled?

Important note: It doesn't matter who is at fault for a stalled or lost lead. These are unprecedented times. When you approach Sales about the desire to recycle stalled or lost leads, they might push back. Reassure them that you only have the best intent. You might consider using language like this in your approach to Sales:

> *"As a result of the instability this year, many of the leads we passed to you might have stalled because of factors outside of your control. What's happening at the lead's company, what's happening in our industry, or what's happened in the economic environment are all factors. Let us help you stay in touch with them and attempt to re-engage them. When they re-engage, we will pass them back to you."*

As for what to do once you have approval to recycle the leads, there are several strategies you can use. One strategy is to survey those leads. Once you've identified the leads that have had no forward progression within a reasonable timeframe (90 days is suitable for most), execute a single question survey from your company or pay an outside marketing agency to execute it on your behalf. What you're hoping to do is to reach out to the prospect and ask them one question, "How was your experience with our company?" This single question will more than likely get you several responses. One of the things that helps with the survey is a little goodwill. Extend an incentive for them to participate in the survey.

I've seen several different incentives work, whether it's a $5 or $10 gift card to Starbucks or a $25 Amazon card. The only advice here is to make sure you budget effectively for a significant response. Keep in mind, many of the industries might have gift policies. Anything under $25 is often safe. You might be able to extend it to $50, but once you get above $50, you run the risk of violating corporate gift policies.

Some of them might say, "Hey, I never spoke with anyone, but I am still interested." It could be that they spoke with someone and are still interested despite not getting the follow up they requested. Another option might be, "Hey, I decided to purchase somewhere else." Of course, that leads to a follow-up question of why? Maybe they are no longer in the market, and that could be for a few reasons, but the follow-up questions could be related to budget availability, or decision timeline. The final is, "Hey, I don't even know who you are. I don't know your company." That's probably a reflection of wherever this lead was sourced from. Remember to be kind to yourself. Your team was busy doing whatever they could to generate a large quantity of leads before there was an agreed upon lead definition of what a qualified, sales-ready lead should look like and organizational alignment on quality over quantity. You were under a lot of pressure to send as many leads as possible. Regardless, follow up on responses appropriately to keep the lead engaged and identify if there is a need and interest in speaking with Sales.

If you execute the survey strategy, make sure that you can update your records in CRM and in your marketing automation platform, and inform the original lead owner of the outcome of that survey. Ideally, you're not operating in spreadsheets everywhere, but if you are, it's probably best to use a collaborative spreadsheet capability, whether it's Smartsheets or Google Sheets, something that would allow you to update in real time while also sharing that insight with Sales. If the lead decides to re-engage with you, make sure you train your sales team how to pursue those leads that are recycled. Make sure the sales rep understands how to reference the survey results in the call.

Next, evaluate your database, identify leads that have been disqualified. Look closely at the disqualification reasons. Identify and prioritize which of those leads make sense to recycle. Based on the disqualification and lost reasons, develop individual marketing strategies to re-engage them based on what you know about them, about where they're at in the decision-making process, and what they know about your offering. For example, if you know that the person has left the company, you could ask your team or an agency partner to strategically find the replacement of that person and engage them by acknowledging that "others in their organization expressed interest in your solutions and they might be interested as well".

If the lead had engaged with a high value piece of content on a specific topic, you could send them a related topic and be explicit about how the new piece of content relates to the content they previously engaged with. Make sure you enable targeting for your website visitors based on certain pages. Continue to stay in front of them through retargeting until they're ready to talk or indicate a sales readiness. If they selected a competing solution, remember that buyer's remorse is a real thing. Continue to communicate with them in a thoughtful way so that they know your company is still here to support them. "We understand that you made a decision to go with a competitor. We'd like to continue to send you valuable tips and tools, smart and helpful content. Should you ever change your mind, just know that we appreciate and value your business and would welcome an opportunity to re-engage with you."

While the value of each lead differs, stalled leads have the potential to become customers and increase the profitability of your company. Depending on your average revenue value of a deal, recycling stalled leads can add hundreds of thousands or even millions to your pipeline. Leave no lead behind.

CHAPTER 9:

Invest in Sales Productivity

Years ago, I was sitting with the CMO of a global Fortune 100 company presenting recommendations for how to improve their return on marketing spend. He asked if there was anything else that his team could do to improve alignment with Sales as he had noticed some tension over whether there was enough leads in the pipeline to achieve the revenue forecast for the remainder of the year. His team had been meeting the goals established at the beginning of the year, but the leads weren't converting at the rate they had projected. Sales was having a harder time hitting their numbers and the tension was building. I asked the CMO what his team was doing to help Sales convert marketing-generated leads or to enable Sales to generate their own leads. I'll never forget his response.

He told me that his team's job was to build brand awareness, loyalty, and to attract and engage the right buyers to generate enough quality leads to fuel the sales pipeline. That's it. At the end of the day, what Sales did with those leads was their responsibility and outside his team's lane. If Sales needed help converting leads and closing opportunities to hit their numbers, the investments needed for that support should come out of their budget. Particularly because the Sales budget was exponentially larger than the Marketing budget.

I was floored. Since I had a decent working relationship with the CMO, I decided to not filter my reaction. My response to him was, 'your very large and expensive team spends $9 million on trade shows to generate leads. My guess is that's a lot of work for your organization, and there's probably a lot of stress that goes along with managing such a large number of events globally. With your current lead conversion rates, if you don't start caring about what happens to those leads after they're passed to Sales, your successor will. In the meantime, you might as well save everyone the hassle of your large events calendar and throw the $9 million in the trash bucket.' He was understandably shocked. While I certainly wasn't serious about throwing $9 million away, that's effectively what he was doing.

He was throwing $9 million away because he felt like his organization's responsibility ended the moment a lead was passed over to Sales. As I've shown you throughout this book, that is not true. Marketing is responsible for both creating demand and making sure that demand converts into profitable revenue. The good news is that he recognized the opportunity and reallocated some of his spend to sales enablement. He and his team did such an amazing job of transforming marketing from a cost center to a profitable revenue engine in partnership with Sales. He's a great example of a marketer that demonstrated his ability to be a business driver by leveraging marketing resources to maximize sales productivity.

The good news is that you can do the same by simply repurposing what you probably already have in your marketing toolkit. Most marketers have buyer insights, marketable data, email templates, automation tools, and content that can be leveraged by Sales with proper training.

Buyer insights—Marketers often invest in voice of customer research to understand the needs, wants, motivations, and core jobs of their target buyer personas. As an extension of that research, many marketers also map out the buying journey for their solutions and use those insights to develop effective messaging and offer strategies. All these insights would be very valuable to Sales if you provide training on how to use the insights to have effective selling conversations.

Additionally, when you're passing leads over to Sales, include any insights about why the lead was deemed qualified and sales ready. This includes any of the buying behaviors that that person might have exhibited, the channel they engaged in, the details of the content they consumed, the tactics that they responded to, as well as any past purchasing history. If you package and deliver these insights along with the lead to the sales rep without requiring twenty clicks through CRM screens, you will have a significant impact on their effectiveness and improve conversion rates.

Marketable data—Because marketing effectiveness depends on our ability to identify and reach prospects, Marketers invest a significant portion of their budgets developing their databases to be more accurate and complete. If you have invested in a data enrichment or intent monitoring platforms, many of these same platforms often have cost effective add-ons to support go-to-market planning, territory planning, account management and lead pursuit activities. For example, the same database you use to enrich records and screen leads against targeting criteria can also be used to help a seller reach the lead through different channels. For example, if a lead provides you with a phone number or email address and the sales rep struggles to connect with the lead, they can use the add-on product to identify the social media profiles to connect in a different channel.

Email templates—Converting leads depends on the timeliness of sales follow up. Speed of lead follow-up can make or break your close rate. Think about it. Most of the time, you're just one of the solutions a prospect is considering. You'll be fighting all your competitors for the sale. And if you don't respond as fast as possible, a competitor will beat you to it and almost always get the sale instead of you. This is true for both simple products and highly technical, complex solutions. One of the things that marketers fail to recognize is how difficult it is for a sales rep to write email copy. In fear of screwing up their one opportunity to engage the lead, your sales rep might write and rewrite the same email repeatedly for days. When the email is finally sent, it's three pages long because they don't know email best practices and are afraid to leave anything out. Not everyone can write a compelling email quickly like an experienced marketer. If you want to maximize lead conversion, provide your sales reps with customizable email templates for your most common lead sources. For example, if leads are generated through webinars, invest a little extra effort in the development of your webinar program to include with the development of an email template that can be used for lead follow-up.

Automation tools—Many industry-leading marketing automation platforms offer add-on products that extend simple email automation capabilities to sales users. This will not only save the sales reps a lot of time sending one email at a time, it also provides them with email performance tracking. For Salesforce's Pardot, the add-on is called Salesforce Engage. For Oracle's Eloqua, the add-on is called Prospect Profiler. For Adobe's Marketo, the add-on is called Sales Connect. The sales rep selects the appropriate email template for their selling scenario, customizes it for the lead then selects the record(s) they want to send the email to—all with just a few clicks of a mouse. In addition to email tracking, they also offer real time alerts for when the lead has engaged with the email and any associated content.

If your sellers are struggling to effectively manage all their leads while cultivating their own network of contacts, there are tools like Salesloft and High Velocity Sales that take the guesswork out of lead nurturing and opportunity management. These platforms help sellers stay in front of their leads by orchestrating every call, every email, every meeting, and every interaction with all activities automatically synced back to CRM to streamline the sales process. Tools like these help sellers engage with more authentic, personalized interactions across all points of the customer journey — from the first lead response through the post-sale experience.

This same platform provides Marketing with end-to-end visibility to the activities being executed to effectively convert leads. Once you unlock the secrets of your most effective sales reps, you can then build sales cadences to accelerate lead conversion. If you're not familiar with sales cadences, here's an example: On day one, you send a lead follow-up email. On day three, you pick up the phone and call. On day ten, if they didn't reply to the email and they didn't answer your phone calls, send another follow-up email. The system prompts the sales rep with the activity that needs to happen that day ensuring that they stay in front of their leads consistently, nothing gets dropped or left behind.

Content -To enable the buyer's entire journey, marketers develop high value content in a variety of formats to be delivered through different channels. Some of this content can be repurposed into assets that support the sales process. For example, the interactive self-assessment tools and return on investment calculators and product comparison charts typically found on your website could be used by sales reps to advance opportunities and close deals.

Audit your content library to identify which assets could be used by sellers to convert leads into sales. Align the assets to the appropriate buying audience and sales stage by thinking about what the customer is trying to learn at each stage of their buyer's journey and your sales process. In short, what question are you answering for them or what should they know to make an informed buying decision? Once you've aligned your existing assets, determine what needs to be updated or repurposed to be suitable for a sales conversation. Make the changes then conduct training on what and when to send to prospective customers.

Smart marketers take it one step further and invest their resources in an artificial intelligence powered sales enablement technology that can proactively surface recommended content for sellers to increase buyer engagement and close deals faster. The same technology enables sellers to customize pitches and proposals to create competitive differentiation and win a greater percentage of deals. The robust analytics simultaneously help sellers replicate the behaviors of top performers and marketers understand content usage and effectiveness.

Sales enablement technology providers range in sophistication from Seismic to Highspot and Showpad. The return on investments on sales enablement have had a greater impact on lead conversion and yielded the highest return on investment than any other marketing investment I've ever made because it simultaneously improves marketing and sales productivity.

Remember that more than 98% of all marketing-generated leads never result in revenue for their organization. To stop the waste, jumpstart your demand engine and grow revenue quickly, help Sales convert a greater percentage of the demand that Marketing is already creating.

THE REVENUE
RAMP

Phase 4: **Propel**

Propelling your organization to growth
by improving marketing effectiveness,
filling the pipeline and maximizing
conversion to drive business impact.

CHAPTER 10:

Eliminate Random Acts of Marketing for Impact

Now that we have established core operating principles for your team, fixed the leaks in your revenue pipeline, shined the light on your organization's wall of shame, improved your relationships with Sales and IT, developed a roadmap for how to mature your processes, gained acceptance on lead definitions, established an integrated view of the Marketing and Sales pipeline, and built an enabling infrastructure to maximize productivity, it is time to execute a powerful strategy to propel your organization forward. It's time to eliminate random acts of marketing.

What IS a random act of marketing, exactly? Random acts of marketing include tactics that:

- Are not aligned to business priorities, goals, target audiences.

- Do not have a plan for how it will be measured, responses will be handled, or what is next.
- Can be described as something that "just needs to get out/done today" to check a box.
- Looks like a marketer is flailing, desperate for something to happen.
- Is referred to as a "test" but without any plan for what we're trying to learn or what we'll do with the findings.
- When received, would elicit the following responses from the recipient:
  - Who is this company?
  - How did I get on this list?
  - Why are they sending me an invite for an event next week, especially when I live in a different State?
  - Why are they sending me a message written for an IT role? Don't they know that I'm in a Marketing role?

Simply stated, it's any tactic, or piece of content, without a plan for what's next from the recipient's perspective.

Here's why random acts of marketing are holding your organization back from achieving its fullest potential:

- They deliver a confusing experience for your customers.
- They lead to high opt-out rates. Marketers often experience shrinking databases as a result.
- They cost more money to execute; does not benefit from volume discounts.
- They consume more resources to execute; lots of duplicative work.

- They distract the team from work of strategic importance; barely able to keep up with the avalanche of one-off requests.
- They do not create any sort of momentum; often the magic of conversion is in the repetition and mix of messages.
- They tend to ignore long-term leads; wasted opportunities.

To eliminate random acts of marketing, you must **SEE, PLAN, EXECUTE,** and **INVEST** differently than you have in the past.

First, you've got to SEE differently.

Seeing differently requires establishing a clear view of what an ideal buyer's journey looks like from your buyer's perspective. Put yourself in their shoes, understand how they search for, evaluate and buy the solutions you have to offer. Understand what an ideal buying experience would look like from their perspective. And then develop a plan for how your organization will deliver those experiences.

Secondly, you must PLAN differently.

If you don't have a plan for what's next from the recipient's perspective, it doesn't go out. It's as simple as that.

Here are four considerations for planning the ideal buyer's journey:

Consideration #1: Visual identity. How do you ensure that the customer's experience with your brand is consistent, regardless of the channel or the stage of the relationship with you?

Consideration #2: Messaging and content. What are the key messages at every stage of the buyer's journey? What content assets map to each one of those stages in the buyer's journey? Do they make sense from the buyer's perspective?

Consideration #3: Delivery channels. What are the different channels that the buyer wants to meet you in, and how are you going to bring those messages to life in those delivery channels? Are you findable in their preferred channels? Are you delivering the experience they'd expect in that channel?

Consideration #4: Always-on experiences. Let's be honest. Amazon has spoiled us. We live in the age of consumer control. Buyers want answers to their questions now, in their moment of need. How are you leveraging the prospect's digital body language to inform the next message along that buyer's journey with the intent of accelerating the time to decision? Are you designing enabling ecosystems as opposed to planning one program or tactic at a time? Are you leveraging retargeting to stay in front of the prospects that did not convert into sales-ready leads? Retargeting will help your organization become omnipresent in the minds of your buyers.

Third, you must EXECUTE differently.

Execution needs to be done programmatically, not one tactic at a time. Always-on campaigns can sometimes contain dozens of tactics that can quickly become an administrative nightmare if managed one tactic at a time. It might take more time to plan and execute it as one unified ecosystem or one package. This is the reason we focused first on generating some quick wins by recycling stalled and lost leads. Use this runway to build and deploy your always-on campaigns. You will deliver a more cohesive customer experience and drive better results to accelerate revenue.

Finally, you must INVEST differently.

All things start with data and roll downhill from there. You can spend millions on the best creative and most compelling messaging and offers but it's useless if it cannot reach your buyer. Invest in continuous data management, standardization and enrichment to support profiling, targeting, and segmentation. For example, you cannot execute on any sort of relevant message for a unique buyer persona if you're unable to segment your database by buyer persona, title, function or organization level.

Once you've addressed the gaps in your data, invest in streamlined, automated lead assignment and distribution. Too many organizations cut corners or overcomplicate lead assignment. It's shocking to me how so many organizations that attempt to manually assign and distribute leads or overcomplicate the process where the turnaround time takes days or weeks. Once a lead is identified as qualified and sales-ready, you should be able to assign, route, and notify the recipient that they have a lead to pursue within minutes. If not, make solving this a priority for your organization. Remember time kills the value of leads.

CHAPTER 11:

Prove Your Impact

According to The Fournaise Marketing Group's 2012 Global Marketing Effectiveness Program,[14] 80% of CEOs admit that they do not really trust and are not very impressed by the work done by marketers. In comparison, 90% of the same CEOs trust and value the opinion and work of their CFOs and CIOs. And the cause? CEOs believe that CMOs are often too disconnected from the short, mid, and long-term financial realities of the company. While 71% of CEOs believe that CMOs are focused on investing in the latest marketing technologies to generate demand, Marketing is still failing to deliver business impact. I disagree. Unless Marketing plays zero role in demand generation, Marketing is delivering business impact. The real problem is that CMOs are failing

---

[14] Watts, K. (2012) 80% of CEOs Do Not Really Trust Marketers. Fournaise Group. Retrieved from: https://www.fournaisegroup.com/ceos-do-not-trust-marketers/

to **PROVE** business impact. The story Marketing is telling is impacting their credibility as business drivers.

Here is a four-step process for proving business impact and strengthening your credibility:

1. Confirm Marketing's purpose and role in the organization.
2. Establish direct linkage between sales and marketing pipelines and performance
3. Identify your stakeholders, what metrics matter to them and deliver reporting that works best for them.
4. Learn how to report properly.

Earlier in this book, we shared strategies to gain alignment on Marketing's role in revenue generation and establish direct linkage between sales and marketing performance with an integrated view of the marketing and sales pipelines. Now it's time to develop an approach to measurement and reporting that will tell a story of accountability, prove business impact and strengthen your credibility as a business driver.

Effective marketing measurement is a process that essentially includes three main phases: **PREPARE, EXECUTE,** and **OPTIMIZE.**

Phase 1: Prepare. Identify your stakeholders, understand their role in the organization, their KPIs and the marketing metrics that matter most to them. Uncover the primary questions they have about marketing performance. These questions will serve as the basis for your reporting goals. Establish clear linkage between reporting goals and business goals. Finalize a list of your KPIs and the related metrics that will need to be tracked to reliably report on performance.

Phase 2: Execute. To effectively design your reports, think through the following questions:

- Who's the audience for the report?
- What's the goal of the report?
- What decisions will they be making with the data?
- What are the formulas you'll use to calculate performance?
- What will be your sources of data for each element of the formulas?
- If the data comes from multiple technologies and databases, how will you aggregate the data for the report?
- What's the measurement timeframe for the report?
- Is it a single snapshot in time?
- Is it a comparison between two different timeframes?
- Is it a rolling average?

Design and create a mockup of the reports for stakeholder feedback. Incorporate the feedback into design then build the production version. Begin testing the data as it flows into your reports. Validate that the data communicates the goal of the report.

Phase 3: Optimize. Once the reports are tested, you'll want to focus on driving user adoption and on-going optimization. Do not just assume that if you build it, they will come. Provide training on how to access and interpret the reports. Also, don't train the organization to ignore the reports and dashboards you've built by failing to use them yourself. If you're giving a presentation that contains an update on progress or performance, access the reports themselves and reference the key points there. Track the utilization of the reports you've built. Solicit feedback on the reports for ongoing optimization. Retire reports that are no longer useful.

No discussion can be had about proving marketing impact or "going on the hook for a revenue number" without talking about revenue attribution. How are you currently assigning revenue generated to your marketing investments?

When it comes to revenue attribution, there are three things to keep in mind:

1. There is no such thing as one perfect revenue attribution model. Every single model has trade-offs. The only perfect model that exists is the one that answers the question you're asking.
2. Marketing will need to secure buy-in from C-Suite on which revenue attribution models make the most sense for your organization. If you don't do this first, stakeholders will question the validity of your reporting simply because they don't understand and/or agree with how revenue was attributed.
3. As you advance your capabilities and execute more sophisticated campaigns and programs, revenue attribution will grow increasingly complex. Make sure that the infrastructure you are building has a strong foundation to support your organization's reporting needs.

While I encourage you to read as much as you can on the available models for revenue attribution, here is an overview of the most used attribution models used by marketers:

First touch attribution model: 100% of the revenue is assigned to the very first marketing touchpoint that either sourced the record or touched the record before it became a sale. First touch is very simple to implement and understand, but it fails to credit any later stage touches. This model is ideally suited for identifying the tactics that were most effective at adding net new leads to the database. Over time, this model could be used to justify eliminating lead nurturing and recycling strategies even though they typically drive the greatest conversion and highest return on investment. Why? Longer-term lead nurturing and recycling programs have nothing to do with the first touchpoint.

Last touch attribution model: 100% of the revenue is assigned to the last marketing touchpoint before the lead was deemed qualified and sales-ready; the moment before it was passed over to Sales. Last touch is good for identifying which assets are most effective at converting an inquiry into a qualified, sales-ready lead. If too much emphasis is placed here, any asset or tactic that is effective in building brand awareness or initially attracting a prospect will be deemed ineffective and potentially cut from the marketer's tool kit.

Even spread model: This model applied the revenue generated from a sale to all the marketing touchpoints along the lifecycle of the lead. Whether someone interacted with a blog post, an interactive total cost of ownership calculator, or attended an event or a webinar, this model is flawed in that it implies every touchpoint equally contributed to the lead conversion. Marketers know that registering and attending a webinar is not the same thing as reading a blog post.

U shaped model: This model gives equal credit to the first and last marketing touchpoints. U-shaped aligns the goals of generating new leads and converting them, but it straddles two opposing pieces of the funnel and it misses everything in the middle that could have kept your organization in front of your prospect and cultivated a preference for your brand. While closer to accurate in weighting key events, the risk here is that it could lead to under-investing in retargeting or nurture strategies.

W shaped model: This model places the highest weight on the first marketing touchpoint, middle touchpoint (which prompted it to become a qualified opportunity), and last touchpoint before it became a closed sale. W-shape includes activities throughout the funnel, straddles middle points, but the aggregate report is much harder to interpret. Many marketers claim that this model results in shaky, unreliable data.

Time decay model: Time decay gives increasing credit to the marketing touchpoints closer to the later stage of that lead's life cycle. More credit is given to the marketing touchpoint that pushed a lead over a conversion point towards a final decision. For example, the lead could have read an article, interacted with a product comparison tool, read a case study then completed a total cost of ownership calculator along their lead lifecycle. The revenue will be attributed to across all touchpoints but weighting increases as it approaches the final conversion. Time decay is great in theory but is flawed too. It assumes that all sales cycles advance in a linear fashion. Unfortunately, nothing really happens in a nice, neat, linear fashion. Thinking about 2020, how many times do you think prospects started, stopped, stalled, paused, or restarted?

Again, there is no such thing as one perfect revenue attribution model. Every single model has trade-offs. The only perfect model that exists is the one that answers the question you're trying to answer. The good news? There are many marketing performance management platforms to choose from that will provide you with the ability to apply different attribution models based on the question you're trying to answer. Here are a few: Hive 9, Anaplan, Allocadia, Aprimo and Bizible.

Effective measurement and reporting will drive cross-functional alignment on the expectations of Marketing for your organization. They're also key to demonstrating accountability for performance and business impact. As you demonstrate progress towards goals, continued performance improvements and prove business impact, you'll strengthen your credibility as a business driver. You'll earn the trust of your peers by eliminating the complexity and uncertainty often associated with Marketing. You'll also be able to demonstrate clear linkage between marketing investments and revenue growth. A meaningful first step in changing the perception of Marketing from a cost center to a profitable revenue engine.

CONCLUSION

You've just finished reading this book, and you might feel a little overwhelmed and stuck. Remember how to eat an elephant? One bite at a time. More specifically, one phase at a time. There are four simple phases of work to build your Revenue RAMP: **REVIEW, ALIGN, MOBILIZE** and **PROPEL**.

I suggest you start with phase 1: **REVIEWING** your processes to uncover gaps and opportunities. Once you've completed phase 1, you'll move on to phase 2—**ALIGNING** Sales & Marketing around the key drivers of revenue generation. Then you'll move on to phase 3—**MOBILIZING** your organization to quickly fix the leaks in your demand pipeline and secure some quick wins. Finally, you'll move to phase 4—**PROPELLING** your organization to growth by improving marketing effectiveness, filling the pipeline and maximizing lead conversion to drive business impact. Executing the simple steps using the phased approach described in this book will help you eliminate waste, improve sales conversion rates, and unlock the potential of your organization to accelerate growth. This can be accomplished all without stretching your team too thin, compromising lead quality, begging for more resources, or damaging your relationship with Sales.

Most marketers can effectively navigate an entire career without struggling through a crisis. This year, no matter where we were in the world, all marketers faced a crisis that effectively rendered all marketing plans useless and irrelevant, wasted significant portions of their budget in delayed or cancelled events, fundamentally changed the way customers bought, and increased pressure on marketing to generate more leads at a time when their demand engine came to a screeching halt. Marketers with companies that were able to pivot quickly with new business models to either capitalize on opportunities or protect themselves from further loss, were also faced with figuring out how to align and enable these new models seemingly overnight in a chaotic environment.

For marketers that were already struggling to earn a seat at the table and be viewed as credible business drivers, you may have been asked to freeze or reduce your marketing spend. Gartner has been surveying CMOs and CFOs quarterly since the start of the pandemic and have confirmed that many marketers have experienced multiple cuts in their budget through the year and going into 2021. When organizations finally realized that the pandemic was in fact going to shut down the economy, the first real cut was, on average, 11% of a marketer's budget. At the midpoint of the year, CFO's said they returned to marketing and took another 14% of their dollars. That is a 25% budget cut in one year and at the same time, you more than likely had a significant portion frozen in negotiations with event exhibitors that were struggling to hold on to the revenues from the events they had planned for the year.

If the economy doesn't support a rapid recovery where businesses experience what feels like a V-Shaped recovery, CFOs are indicating that marketers can expect another budget cut going into 2021. With fewer resources and increasing pressure, marketers don't have the luxury of just doing more activities or sending more leads over to sales. We will have to see, plan, execute and invest differently than we ever have.

The good news is if you work through this program to build your revenue RAMP for the business, you will have cross-functional support to jumpstart your stalled demand engine, return the business to growth and prove your impact as a business driver. This program helped my team deliver high quality leads that sales valued, helped my company manage through the massive disruption in our key markets, set us up for long term success and has helped solidify my reputation as a business driver. It will work for you too.

Ok, it's time to get to work. Start with establishing operating principles with your team and shore up your response channels so you're not wasting any demand. There is an odd silver lining to this challenging year in that Sales is probably more receptive to your support and new marketing strategies.

You have a unique opportunity to develop a more agile, cost-effective, scalable and impactful revenue engine with the help and advocacy of your Sales organization. Go build your Revenue RAMP.

If you need any help as you build your Revenue RAMP, please don't hesitate to reach out. If this book helped you, I'd love to know that too. My email address is lisacole@therevenueramp.com or connect with me on LinkedIn.

ACKNOWLEDGEMENTS

Whenever I read a new book, I jump first to the acknowledgements section to see if the author reveals the catalyst for their work and who they credit for their work's evolution. I love to see the author's "WHY" behind their book.

The catalyst for my work happened in 1994. I was an account executive for a Fortune 500 telecommunications company and desperately trying to fill my pipeline with enough sales opportunities to achieve my quota and keep my job. After a few weeks, it was clear that I was going to have to build that pipeline without any help from my "Sink or Swim" Sales Manager and our shockingly internally-focused marketing organization - both of which loved to blame each other for their problems. Despite their lack of support and the toxic environment they nurtured, I achieved quota thanks to my personal network. While it was an incredibly stressful time in my life, I am grateful to have experienced the dysfunction in that company and the pain of trying to achieve sales quotas without any meaningful support from Marketing. That experience helped me find my "WHY" early on, inspired my life's work and led to the development of the Revenue RAMP framework outlined in this book. Since none of this could have been done without the support and effort of others, I'd like to take this opportunity to acknowledge their work. If I have missed anyone, I apologize; any omissions are unintentional.

First and foremost, I have been blessed with many inspiring mentors, innovative clients and supportive peers who gave me countless opportunities to develop my leadership, marketing, and sales skills. In particular, I'd like to acknowledge Virginia Sambuco, Jill Linsenberg, Joe Giovino, Robert Mason, John Zell, Penny Carroll, Jeff Zeigler, Charles DallAqua, Rob Solomon, Todd Davison, Heather Davison, Terry Flaherty, Bruce Brien, Corey Livingston, Lauren McQuade, Barb Goworowski, Andrew Mahler, Peter Wroblewski, Kevin Coe, Debbie Murphy, Ann Hewitt, Patty Olsen, Nora Conroy and Mark Hussey. Thank you for your trust, coaching, guidance, and inspiration through the years. You paved the way for me and my work.

I also want to thank all my team members, past and present. Your hard work, dedication, brilliance, and collaborative nature raise the bar for how marketers are judged. You handle so much so well, and with unparalleled professionalism. I'd like to thank Val Vazquez, Mary Gruber, Kate Kirwan, Bobby Wilson, Kim Thomas, Costa Neofotistos, Betsy LaSalle, Tim Mulcrone and Courtney Radziewicz. While our career journeys have taken us in different directions, I am proud of the work we did together and hope that our career paths cross again in the future. Until then, please know that I'm still cheering you on from the stands.

Speaking of cheerleaders, I'd like to thank Kimberley (Red) Hampson, Tara Cardinal, Melissa Gentry Marder and Kim Duffey for their unconditional love and support. There are few whose words of advice I value more than yours. While your communication styles are wildly different, you always know the right thing to say to help me overcome fears and make smart decisions. One of which was to finally publish this long overdue book!

Finally, I am most thankful for my family. Mom and Dad, you let go of your dreams and sacrificed a ton so that I can achieve mine. I cannot say enough thanks to you in this lifetime for your contribution to my life. For my children, Hadley, Jacob and Savannah, your love for reading helped me understand why it was so important to finally finish this book. Lindsey, thank you for being the guiding light when life threw me in the darkest of corners. If I've made the right choices in life, it is because I had you to help me make them. Thank you for being my person and for supporting my career. I can't wait to see what our party of five accomplishes together through the years. Love you to the moon and back.

AUTHOR BIO

Author and award-winning marketer, Lisa Cole brings more than 20 years' experience transforming marketing functions into scalable, predictable, and accountable growth engines for industry leading B2B organizations. What started as an obsession with Marketing & Sales alignment became a passion for helping marketers change the perception of marketing and establish themselves as business drivers. In addition to delivering hundreds of millions in marketing sourced revenue for organizations, Lisa's inspiring, transformational work led to two awards: SiriusDecisions' 2018 ROI Award and Demand Gen Report's 2018 B2B Innovator Award for C-Suite Strategy. She is also the mother of three children, so leading a global marketing organization is the second most challenging & rewarding thing she does in life.

INDEX

G

Gartner, 15, 150
GDPR regulations, 49
ghosting, 54
"going on the hook for a
    revenue number", 144
Google search, 100
Google Sheets, 122
go-to-market strategy, 53, 73,
    92–93, 104

H

Harvard Business Review, 30
High Velocity Sales, 129
Hive 9, 147
"How do you eat an
    elephant?", 70–71

I

immature organizations
    marketing activity, 59–60
inbound channels, 45
inbound inquiries, 61, 76
inbound phone calls, 42
incentives
    for survey participation, 120
    integrated compensation
        system, 62
influenced revenues, 17,
    60, 72, 80
Information
    Technology (IT), 109
    marketing and, 104–105
in-person events, 43
inquiries, 26
    handling, 28
    implicit/explicit criteria, 110
    inbound, 61, 76
    into qualified,
        sales-ready lead, 145
    web, 43
inside sales, 98. *See also* sales

integrated marketing and sales
    pipeline, 61, 79, 81, 87, 88
interactive self-assessment
    tools, 130
investment, in random acts of
    marketing, 139–140
IT. *See* Information Technology

K

key hand-offs, 98
KPI, 62, 142

L

last touch revenue attribution
    model, 145
lead assignment, 40, 41, 114
    engine, 101
lead conversion, 30, 37, 39,
    98, 101, 126
lead criteria, 91
lead definition, 76
    universally accepted, 61
    workshop, 34, 102
lead disposition, 111
lead flow, 111
    diagram, 40
    process map, 112
lead follow-up
    assessment, 40–45
lead generation
    premature, 27
    sources, 100
lead handling processes, 32, 61
    tele-qualification and, 77
lead lifecycle, 18, 32, 39, 41,
    77, 81, 86, 98, 101
lead management, 43, 76, 81
    council, 102
    specialist, 35
lead notification, 42, 44
lead nurturing, 60, 88
lead owner, 121
Lead pursuit time, 91

time decay revenue attribution
model, 146–147
Total Cost of
Ownership (TCO), 95
trade shows, 40, 117
transformational change, 25,
33, 52, 70, 110
Tutu, Desmond, 71

U

universally accepted lead
definition, 61
unsubscribe, 49
user testing, 115
U shaped revenue attribution
model, 146

V

value measurement
metrics, 59–61

Visio, 112
visual identity, 138
V-shaped recovery, 149

W

"wall of shame", 47–54, 135
example, 49–52
wasted demand, 37,
39, 80, 100
web forms, 42, 45, 95
changes in, 115
webinars, 34, 40, 118
web inquiries, 43
"what if" questions, for
sales-readiness, 95
white space analysis, 73
W shaped revenue attribution
model, 146